Y0-CRF-540

Sex and the Seminary:

Preparing Ministers for Sexual Health and Justice

Kate M. Ott, Ph.D., Study Director

© 2009
Religious Institute on Sexual Morality, Justice, and Healing
Union Theological Seminary in the City of New York

ISBN10: 1-893-270-49-1   ISBN13: 978-1-893270-49-7

Contents

List of Tables

Acknowledgements

The Sexuality Education for the Formation of Religious Professionals and Clergy project is the result of a collaborative partnership between Union Theological Seminary and the Religious Institute on Sexual Morality, Justice, and Healing.

The project and report would not be possible without the assistance of Rev. Debra W. Haffner, Director of the Religious Institute, who served as the project consultant. Her past work on the criteria for a sexually healthy religious professional and a sexually healthy congregation are the building blocks of our study. Her careful attention to the survey, evaluation of complex factors, and ability to articulate recommendations has been invaluable.

Religious Institute staff member Tim Palmer, consultant Barbara Jay, and Holly Sprunger of Christian Community provided editing. The report reflects nuance and clarity thanks to their skill and careful attention.

Early on, Rev. Dr. Joseph C. Hough, Jr., former Union Theological Seminary President, committed Union to the project and Rev. Cathlin Baker, former Senior Assistant to the President, devoted time and energy to seeing the project through its first stage. The project continues with the leadership of Dr. Su Yon Pak, Vice President for Institutional Advancement and Rev. Dr. L. Serene Jones, Union's current President.

In the first phase of the project, an advisory committee developed the institutional survey, advised on seminary selection, and reviewed the initial survey results. The committee, willing volunteers and wise practitioners in the fields of seminary education and sexuality, offered guidance with institutional selection and survey frame design.

Members include: Dr. Sarah C. (Sally) Conklin, Associate Professor, Coordinator of Public Health and Health Education Programs at Northern Illinois University; Rev. Dr. Larry Greenfield, Executive Minister of American Baptist Churches of Metro Chicago, former President of Colgate Rochester Seminary; Rev. Dr. Horace L. Griffin, Interim Director of Field Education at General Theological Seminary; Rev. Debra W. Haffner, Director of the Religious Institute on Sexual Morality, Justice, and Healing; Dr. Amy-Jill Levine, E. Rhodes and Leona B. Carpenter Professor of New Testament Studies at the Divinity School and Graduate Department of Religion, Vanderbilt University; Rev. Dr. Jay E. Johnson, Assistant Professor of Theology, Pacific School of Religion; Rabbi Mychal B. Springer, Associate Dean and Director of Field Education of the Rabbinical School at the Jewish Theological Seminary, where she holds the Helen Fried Kirshblum Goldstein Chair in Professional and Pastoral Skills; and Dr. Su Yon Pak, Vice President for Institutional Advancement at Union Theological Seminary.

In addition to the advisory committee, administrators of theological schools, advocacy organizations, and faculty whose efforts represent a significant contribution to sexuality education of seminary students provided feedback and recommendations on the findings. Their questions, comments, and practical experience brought depth and clarity to the findings.

The following additional professionals donated their time to this project: Dr. Ellen T. Armour, E. Rhodes and Leona B. Carpenter Chair in Feminist Theology and Director of the Carpenter Program in Religion, Gender, and Sexuality at Vanderbilt Divinity School; Rev. Dr. Mariah A. Britton, CEO and Founder of Moriah Institute; Rev. Dr. James M. Childs, Jr., Edward C. Fendt Professor of Systematic

Theology at Trinity Lutheran Seminary; Dr. Robert C. Dykstra, Professor of Pastoral Theology at Princeton Theological Seminary; Rev. Dr. Marvin M. Ellison, Bass Professor of Christian Ethics at Bangor Theological Seminary; Rev. Dr. Marie Fortune, Founder and Senior Analyst of FaithTrust Institute; Rev. Matthew Davis Westfox at the Religious Coalition for Reproductive Choice; Dr. Sharon Groves, Religion and Faith Program at the Human Rights Campaign; Dr. Lori Lefkovitz, Sadie Gottesman and Arlene Gottesman Reff Professor of Gender and Judaism and Director, Kolot: The Center for Jewish Women's and Gender Studies at Reconstructionist Rabbinical College; Tisa Lewis, Director of Accreditation and Institutional Evaluation at the Association of Theological Schools; Dr. Pamela Lightsey, Dean of Students at Garret-Evangelical Theological Seminary; Dr. Deborah F. Mullen, Dean of Master's Programs, Associate Professor of Ministry and Historical Studies, and Director of the Center for African American Ministry and Black Church Studies at McCormick Theological Seminary; Dr. William Stayton at Morehouse School of Medicine and the Center for Sexuality and Religion; Rev. Dr. Emilie Townes, Andrew W. Mellon Professor of African American Religion and Theology and Academic Dean at Yale University Divinity School; Michael Underhill, Director of the LGBTQ Religious Studies Center at Chicago Theological Seminary; and, Rev. Dr. Traci West, Associate Professor of Ethics and African American Studies at Drew University.

Finally, no research project would be possible without the commitment of those gathering the data. A word of appreciation is due to the 36 on-site coordinators who added the 120-question survey to their "to-do" list. Completing the survey required contacting multiple faculty members, students, and administrators for bits of information that ultimately provided a portrait of sexuality education in seminaries. These efforts were diligently supported by Religious Institute student interns: Diana Bell, Delfin Bautista, and Katey Zeh.

The initial research, subsequent feedback, and ongoing outreach would not be possible without the generous support of an anonymous funder to whom we are deeply grateful, as well as the Evelyn and Walter Haas, Jr. Fund.

Kate M. Ott, PhD
Study Director
Associate Director, Religious Institute

Executive Summary

Religious leaders have the potential to change society's understanding of sexuality through the power of the pulpit, pastoral care of individuals and families, and their presence in the media, politics, and civil society. At a time when many denominations and faith communities are embroiled in sexuality issues, there is an urgent need for leaders who understand the connections between religion and sexuality.

Seminaries are not providing future religious leaders with sufficient opportunities for study, self-assessment, and ministerial formation in sexuality. They are also not providing seminarians with the skills they will need to minister to their congregants and communities, or to become effective advocates where sexuality issues are concerned.

Sex and the Seminary: Preparing Ministers for Sexual Health and Justice summarizes the findings of a survey by the Religious Institute on Sexual Morality, Justice, and Healing and Union Theological Seminary. Thirty-six U.S. seminaries, representing a range of religious affiliations, institutional structures, geographic locations, and student populations, participated in this investigation of the sexuality education of religious professionals and clergy.

The survey measured participating seminaries according to the *Criteria for a Sexually Healthy and Responsible Seminary,* which was developed by a multifaith group of seminary educators, administrators, and sexuality educators. The survey explored how sexuality is addressed in the curriculum, policy, demographics, and advocacy of each seminary. None of the 36 institutions in this survey met 100% of the criteria; only ten met a majority of them. *Overall, the results point to an overwhelming need for improvement in the sexuality education provided to seminarians and the overall sexual health of the seminary.*

Among the survey's key findings:

Future clergy and other religious professionals can graduate without taking a sexuality course. More than nine in ten of the seminaries surveyed do not require full-semester sexuality and LGBT courses for graduation. Only one seminary requires a course in sexuality issues for religious professionals, and only two require an LGBT/queer studies course.

Courses focusing on sexuality-related issues are often absent from the curriculum. Most of the seminaries in the survey do not offer full-semester sexuality-related courses. Two-thirds do not have a course in sexuality issues for religious professionals. Three-quarters do not have an LGBT/queer studies course. Where courses exist, fewer than one in ten of the seminaries offer them every semester or every year. Only one in six seminaries requires a sexual ethics course.

Women and feminist studies courses are covered much more often than any other sexuality area. The seminaries surveyed are teaching three times as many full-semester courses in women/feminist studies as they are in sexuality issues for religious professionals or LGBT/queer studies. They offer almost three times as many majors, minors, and certificates in women and feminist studies as in sexuality or LGBT/queer studies. Introductory courses cover gender and women in religion two to four times more often than sexuality or LGBT/queer topics.

The coming generation of scholars is not teaching sexuality-related courses. Curricular offerings in sexuality are faculty driven—that is, the availability of courses depends on faculty members being willing to offer them. Most (94%) full-semester sexuality-related courses are being taught either by faculty at the senior professor level or by adjunct professors and lecturers. Junior-level professors seeking tenure-track positions are generally not teaching sexuality-related courses.

There is a stained glass ceiling in seminaries. Two-thirds of the seminaries surveyed have fewer than 40% women faculty, administrative leaders, or board of trustees positions.

There is a need for full inclusion policies. More than half of the seminaries (66%) do not have policies for full inclusion of women. Half do not have policies for full inclusion of gay and lesbian persons (50%). Almost two-thirds do not have full inclusion policies for transgender persons (61%).

Despite these shortfalls, the survey also reveals areas where progress has been made:

- Eight in ten of the institutions surveyed offer learning opportunities (such as classes or workshops) in sexual harassment prevention. More than two-thirds require instruction in sexual harassment prevention for all ministry students, and more than one-third require it of all students. More than nine in ten have sexual harassment policies for faculty, staff, and student relationships.

- Twenty-five percent of seminaries have free-standing centers or programs dedicated to a sexuality-related issue. The existence of the centers results in increased course offerings, workshops, and learning opportunities in sexuality-related topics; faculty positions with a specialization in sexuality-related research; and often greater advocacy on sexuality-related issues.

- Three out of four schools report that members of faculty or senior administrative staff have published on or been featured in the media addressing a sexual justice issue. LGBT issues were the most likely concerns addressed.

- Students are creating their own opportunities for sexuality-related non-curricular experiences. Students were able to participate in events on sexual and reproductive justice at two-thirds of the seminaries, and many of the seminaries offer sexuality-related worship and student advocacy or support groups. Worship opportunities and student advocacy groups are the only categories where LGBT/queer issues are addressed equally to women and feminist studies topics.

- Sexuality issues are often addressed within a framework of intersecting social justice issues, such as economics, environmental issues, racial/ethnic diversity, and disability issues. The majority of faculty teaching sexuality issues for religious professionals or LGBT/queer studies courses and all of the sexuality-related centers address sexuality from racial, ethnic, and cross-cultural perspectives.

Institutional profiles were developed for each seminary based on how they met the criteria for a sexually healthy and responsible seminary. The profiles suggest that even the most committed seminaries could be doing more to prepare their students and promote the sexual well-being of their institutions.

Sexuality Education and Ministerial Formation

Sexuality is a sacred part of life. Clergy and other religious professionals have a unique opportunity, and responsibility, to guide congregations and communities through any number of sexuality-related concerns. Consider the variety of commonplace experiences that demonstrate how clergy encounter sexuality issues in congregational life:

- The education committee begins drafting a sexual abuse prevention policy.
- During pastoral counseling, a congregant tells the minister that he is no longer sexually attracted to his wife.
- A study group explores the ramifications of a new denominational report on sexuality.
- A 15-year-old girl in the church youth group asks her pastor or youth minister for advice on telling her parents she is a lesbian.
- A congregant calls in the middle of the night to say she had her husband arrested for hitting her—again.
- A social action committee conducts a letter-writing campaign to raise funding for family planning services.
- Two youth members of the congregation seek advice from their rabbi because the young woman is pregnant.
- An infertile couple seeks counseling about use of in vitro fertilization.
- Two elderly members of the congregation who have been dating ask the pastor for advice in telling their adult children about their relationship.

Clearly, congregants and others in the community rely on clergy as a source of counseling and guidance when it comes to questions of sexuality. Many perceive religious professionals and clergy, regardless of training or lack thereof, as capable of dealing with marital counseling and sexual dysfunction,[1] teen sexual development and

---

[1] Conklin, S. (2000). "Six Billion and Counting Compel Sexuality Study in Churches." *The Clergy Journal* 76(6), 3-5.

relationships,[2] and family planning decisions.[3] Unfortunately, these perceptions do not always square with the reality of seminary education. And no one understands this better than clergy and seminarians themselves.

Silence and Sexuality

Ideally, clergy and other religious professionals will have formal, graduate-level training that will enable them to become "sexually healthy." As described by Debra Haffner in 2001, sexually healthy religious professionals are "comfortable with their own sexuality, have skills to provide pastoral care and worship on sexuality issues, and are committed to sexual justice in their congregation and society at large."[4] The box [right] provides more information on these ministerial competencies.

According to the Pan American Health Organization, professionals who address sexuality issues should have certain basic training. This includes "basic knowledge of human sexuality, awareness of personal attitudes towards one's own and other people's sexuality which should include a respectful attitude towards persons with different sexual orientations and sexual practices, and basic skills in identifying, and if necessary, referring to the appropriate professional, problems of sexual health."[5] Other professions, such as the medical and counseling fields, instituted required training in preventative and proactive sexuality education after research demonstrated a clear need for and lack of training.[6]

Over the last two decades, a series of studies has reported that seminarians and clergy feel unprepared

Sexually Healthy Religious Professionals Are:

- Knowledgeable about human sexuality;
- Familiar with their tradition's sacred texts on sexuality;
- Able to engage in theological reflection about how best to integrate sexuality and spirituality;
- Able to examine the impact of racism, sexism, heterosexism and homophobia in ministry;
- Trained in pastoral counseling approaches that facilitate resolution of conflict, specifically when dealing with sexual matters, for individuals, families and groups;
- Able to serve as role models, discussing sexual issues with ease and comfort;
- Knowledgeable about their denomination's policies on sexuality;
- Able to speak out for sexual justice within their denomination and in the larger community;
- Skilled in preaching about sexuality-related issues;
- Able to recognize their own personal limitations and boundaries when it comes to handling sexuality issues;
- Able to deal appropriately with sexual feelings that may rise for congregants, and vice-versa.

Debra W. Haffner, *A Time to Build: Creating Sexually Healthy Faith Communities*.

---

[2] Clapp, S., et al. (2002). *Faith Matters*. Fort Wayne, IN: Christian Community/LifeQuest.
[3] Ellison, C.G. & Goodson, P. (1997). "Conservative Protestantism and Attitudes Toward Family Planning in a Sample of Seminarians." *Journal for the Scientific Study of Religion* 36(4), 512–529.
[4] Haffner, Debra W. (2001). *A Time to Build: Creating Sexually Healthy Faith Communities*. Westport, CT: Religious Institute on Sexual Morality, Justice, and Healing, 14.
[5] Pan American Health Organization (2001). Promotion of Sexual Health. Recommendations for Action (Washington, DC: PAHO), 6. See also, Haffner, Debra W. (2001). *A Time to Build: Creating Sexually Healthy Faith Communities*, Westport, CT: Religious Institute on Sexual Morality, Justice, and Healing, 14.
[6] See Schmidt, Karen (2002) "Moving Beyond Fear," *Yale Medicine*, Winter 2002. Yale University School of Medicine; Weiderman, M.W. & Sansone, R.A. (1999) "Sexuality Training for Professional Psychologists: A National Survey of Training Directors in Doctoral Programs and Predoctoral Internships," *Professional Psychology Research and Practice*, 30, 312-317; and, Pope, K.S., Sonne, J.L., & Holroyd, J. (1993) *Sexual Feelings in Psychotherapy: Explorations of Therapists and Therapists-in-training*. Washington, DC: American Psychological Association.

and ill-equipped to deal with a range of sexuality-related issues.[7] A study of Protestant clergy, conducted in the late 1980s and released in 1991 as *Sex in the Parish*, found that clergy are "not clear about roles, rules, possibilities, and limits in the sexual arena."[8] They reported being uncomfortable discussing sexual matters, even with married couples. The goal of the study was to develop a framework for professional sexual ethics, but also helped to articulate the broader implications of sexuality as it relates to ministry. Lebacqz and Barton made connections between theological education and the practice of ministerial sexual ethics:

> What we think is acceptable sexual conduct depends in part on how we define sexuality, and this in turn depends on how we understand God and God's creation. Although clergy are trained theologically and spend much of their lives reflecting on the theological meaning of human life in all its dimensions, this does not guarantee that they will have a clear theological perspective on sexuality.[9]

They concluded that a single framework was not sufficient as nuances arose for particular groups such as women in ministry, single pastors, and gay, lesbian, and bisexual pastors. They recommended components essential to a professional sexual ethic: "account for pastoral power, for sexism and its effect on both pastors and parishioners, for heterosexism and its implications, and for other social and psychological factors that set the stage for sexual behavior." It must also adequately deal with potential for sexual abuse, as well as sexual relations with "honorable intentions."[10]

In 2001, the *Seminary Sexuality Education Survey*, conducted by Sally Conklin with the support of the Center for Sexuality and Religion, investigated how seminary training prepared clergy to address the sexuality-related needs of congregants. She found that 85% of seminaries embedded sexuality content within other seminary courses. Of those, less than half offered stand-alone courses on any sexuality-related topic. Twenty-five percent of the respondents said their school has not attempted to offer sexuality-related experiences due to low priority of topic, lack of expertise or interest among the faculty, and a sense that the content was covered in other venues.[11] The survey concluded that "those preparing for ministry were not helped to understand their own sexual values or behaviors, and where there were courses in sexuality, they were not required or connected to the core curriculum."[12]

In 2004, a survey of graduates between 1992 and 2002 at five evangelical seminaries reported that minimal attention was given to understanding and maintaining sexual health or in managing feelings of sexual attraction in professional contexts. The graduates felt most prepared to deal with "liability issues" such as abuse, privacy, and boundaries, but less prepared for sexually positive developmental/coping skills such as exploration, sharing, understanding, acceptance, encouragement, and frankness. Researchers concluded that incidents of abuse are reduced and graduates are clearer on sexual misconduct, but they do not know what to do with expected feelings of sexual attraction to congregants. Graduates did perceive their faculty members as helpful on an out-of-class basis, moreso than the seminary structure of classes and training.[13]

---

[7] See Richards, D.E. (1992) "Issues of Religion, Sexual Adjustment, and the Role of the Pastoral Counselor" in R. M. Green (Ed.), *Religion and Sexual Health: Ethical, Theological, and Critical Perspectives*. Norwell, MA: Kluwer Academic Publishers; and, Friesen, D.H. (1988) "Sex Education in the Seminary Setting: Its Effects on Attitudes, Knowledge, and Counseling Responses (Doctoral Dissertation, The University of Iowa, 1988). Dissertation Abstracts International, 50(07A).
[8] Lebacqz, Karen & Barton, Ronald (1991) *Sex in the Parish*. Louisville: Westminster/John Knox Press, 8.
[9] Ibid., 11.
[10] Ibid., 16.
[11] Conklin, S. (2001) "Seminary Sexuality Education Survey: Current Efforts, Perceived Need and Readiness in Accredited Christian Institutions," *Journal of Sex Education and Therapy*, 26(4), 301–309. The survey was most often answered by Chief Academic Officer—usually Academic Dean with responses from 69 of 183 Association of Theological Schools Members (30%).
[12] The Center for Sexuality and Religion (2002) Section: The Role of Sexuality Education Within Seminaries in *The Case for Comprehensive Sexuality Education Within the Context of Seminary Human and Theological Formation: A Report of the Ford Foundation*, 8.
[13] Meek, Katheryn Rhoads, et al. (2004) "Sexual Ethics Training in Seminary: Preparing Students to Manage Feelings of Sexual Attraction," *Pastoral Psychology*, 53(1), 63–79.

Restructuring Ministerial Education

Over the past decade, the Association of Theological Schools (ATS) has renewed the focus of theological education to be attentive to aspects of ministerial formation, specifically skills training for the ministry.[16] In 2003, ATS President Daniel O. Aleshire wrote:

> While our scholarly work should be done in the arts traditions, excellence in pastoral work is not defined by excellence in the liberal arts. Our disciplines, for the most part, are clearly anchored in an appropriate intellectual style that is different from the intellectual style that the best of our graduates may use in ministerial practice.[17]

In a 2008 Religious Institute survey of progressive clergy, fewer than four in ten (38%) agreed that their seminary adequately prepared them for dealing with sexuality issues in their congregations. In addition, only one-third (35%) agreed that their seminary adequately prepared them for dealing with LGBT issues in their congregations.[14]

Despite 20 years of consistent findings that seminaries are falling short, most seminaries are still not preparing future religious professionals to address sexuality issues in liturgy, counseling, education, or policy making. There has been a shift toward encouraging, and in some cases requiring, preventative training to reduce sexual abuse—a change that is to be applauded.[15] Yet, as suggested in both *Sex in the Parish* in 1991 and the survey of evangelical seminaries in 2004, if avoidance of abuse or misconduct is the only manner in which students learn about sexuality in ministry, the focus remains on liability and unhealthy sexual behaviors.

Structuring ministerial education to correspond to the needs of the professional life into which students graduate requires a renewed emphasis on experiential learning and on balancing the competition of educational needs across the curriculum. As the ATS Curriculum Standards state, the overarching goal of the theological curriculum "is the development of theological understanding" which includes "acquiring the abilities requisite to the exercise of ministry" in an individual's community of faith.[18]

ATS requires that all accredited schools "seek to assist students in gaining the particular knowledge, appreciation, and openness needed to live and practice ministry effectively in changing cultural and racially diverse settings."[19] Students acquire this "knowledge, appreciation and

[14] Survey of Religious Progressives (2008) Religious Institute on Sexual Morality, Justice, and Healing.

[15] See Robinson, Linda Hansen (2004) "The Abuse of Power: A View of Sexual Misconduct in a Systemic Approach to Pastoral Care," *Pastoral Psychology*, Vol. 52, No. 5, May 2004, 395–404; Brichard, Thaddeus (2000) "Clergy Sexual Misconduct: Frequency and Causation," *Sexual and Relationship Therapy*, 15, 127–139; and, Fortune, M. M. (1991) *Is Nothing Sacred? When Sex Invades the Pastoral Relationship*. San Francisco: Harper.

[16] See Aleshire, Daniel O. (2008) *Earthen Vessels: Hopeful Reflections on the Work and Future of Theological Schools*. Grand Rapids, MI: Wm. B. Eerdmans Publishing Company; Schuth, K. (1999) *Seminaries, Theologates, and the Future of Church Ministry: An Analysis of Trends and Transitions*. Collegeville, MN: The Liturgical Press; Hough, J. C., Jr. (1995) "Future Pastors, Future Church: The Seminary Quarrels," *The Christian Century*, 112(18), 564–567; King, G. B. (1995) "Trends in Seminary Education" in K. B. Bedell (Ed.), *Yearbook of American & Canadian Churches 1995*. Nashville, TN: Abingdon Press.

[17] Aleshire, Daniel (2003) "What Matters in Good MDiv Curricula?" Presented at the Consultation on Designing MDiv Curriculum, The Association of Theological Schools.

[18] The Association of Theological Schools (2006) "Degree Program Standards," Bulletin 47, Part 1, Standard A, section A.4.1.1. Pittsburgh, PA.

[19] Ibid., section A.2.5

openness" when theological scholarship "is enhanced by active engagement with the diversity and global extent of [the] wider publics, and … a consciousness of racial, ethnic, gender, and global diversities."[20] It is important for students to reflect on how diverse racial and ethnic cultures and variations in religious traditions have affected their own sexualities and those of the people they will be called to serve. Currently, ATS standards do not recognize active engagement or consciousness of diverse sexualities and gender identities, which are also present in most religious settings.[21]

According to ATS, the primary goals of a ministry degree program "should take into account: knowledge of the religious heritage; understanding of the cultural context; growth in spiritual depth and moral integrity; and capacity for ministerial and public leadership."[22] Sexuality-

related issues are present in each of these four areas and must be dealt with explicitly to best prepare religious professionals and clergy for ministry careers.

Besides accreditation standards, denominational ordination requirements also shape the structure of ministerial education. Some denominations have reviewed their ordination criteria and made statements regarding the need for sexuality education of their future clergy, but most have yet to implement any specific requirements. For example, as a result of the process in the United Church of Christ called "Ask the Churches About Faith and Sexuality: A Needs Assessment Survey for Program Development," seven recommendations were suggested, including "equip clergy to respond to human sexuality-related needs." The report states:

---

[20] The Association of Theological Schools (2006) "Degree Program Standards," Bulletin 47, Part 1, Standard A, section A.3.2.1.3. Pittsburgh, PA.
[21] Palmer, Timothy, et al. (2007) *A Time to Seek: Study Guide on Sexual and Gender Diversity, Westport, CT: Religious Institute on Sexual Morality, Justice, and Healing.*
[22] The Association of Theological Schools (2006) "Degree Program Standards," Bulletin 47, Part 1, Standard A, section A.2.0. Pittsburgh, PA.

Clergy and laity alike expect that local pastors will make themselves available to respond to the human-sexuality-related needs of persons in congregations and communities. To provide such assistance, clergy should be trained by seminaries and through continuing-education opportunities. Members of clergy look to the seminaries, conferences, and national church bodies to provide this training.[23]

The Presbyterian Church, USA made similar statements in its 1991 denominational statement on "Human Sexuality." With regard to ordained pastors, the report notes "the person called to care for the well-being of members of a congregation, a pastor must be spiritually sensitive and sexually self-aware, with responsible good judgment about his or her interactions with other people." In response to the training and education needed for clergy, the report states:

> Seminarians and all clergy need in-depth training dealing with boundaries between professional and personal relationships, sexuality, sensitivity to their own sexual feelings and those of other people, awareness of the limits of their counseling knowledge and skills, and the effect of stress on clergy.[24]

Before any substantive restructuring of ministerial education can happen, seminaries must recognize that not offering sexuality courses is also a kind of sexuality education. A null curriculum or lack of attention to sexuality can convey a lack of regard for pastoral problems arising from sexuality, while reinforcing the shame and discomfort that often attend sexuality issues.[25]

Criteria for a Sexually Healthy and Responsible Seminary

Given the heightened recognition that clergy influence the sexual lives of those they are called to serve, a sexually healthy and responsible seminary provides training in sexuality issues so that seminary graduates and ordained clergy emerge as trained religious professionals who can deal with the complexity of sexual matters—in a healthy, constructive, and appropriate manner. Formation of religious professionals and clergy will require more than a renewal of the curriculum. It requires an institutional shift toward becoming a sexually healthy and responsible seminary that models respect and dignity for all persons.

The Religious Institute and Union Theological Seminary held a one-day colloquium of prominent seminary leaders to develop the criteria for a sexually healthy and responsible seminary. They began by reviewing previously published work on the characteristics of a sexually healthy religious professional and a sexually healthy faith community. They addressed how the seminary can graduate professionals who have the background, opportunities, and skills to be sexually healthy and responsible. These criteria can serve as a framework for evaluating and guiding seminaries as they seek to better prepare their students for ministry. The criteria are on pages 12 and 13.

[23] Johnson, F. Barker et al., "Ask the Churches about Faith and Sexuality: A UCC Survey of Needs for Program Development." Unpublished report presented to the United Church Board for Homeland Ministries, 22.

[24] Presbyterian Church, USA. (1991) "Response to the Report of the Special Committee on Human Sexuality, Including a Minority Report." Louisville, KY: Office of the General Assembly, Presbyterian Church (USA), 71, 73.

[25] The Center for Sexuality and Religion (2002) *The Case for Comprehensive Sexuality Education Within the Context of Seminary Human and Theological Formation: A Report of the Ford Foundation*, 12.

Criteria for a Sexually Healthy and Responsible Seminary

Religious traditions affirm that sexuality is God's life-giving and life-fulfilling gift. Every member of the clergy will be called upon to address the sexuality needs of the people they serve; yet, only a handful of seminaries in the U.S. are actively preparing their students to assume this important role.

A sexually healthy and responsible seminary is committed to fostering spiritual, sexual, and emotional health for its students, faculty, and staff and providing a safe environment where sexuality issues are addressed with respect, mutuality, and openness.

Every seminary needs to help students address formation issues relating to their own sexuality, understand a range of sexuality issues including scholarship on sexuality and gender, and develop competencies for addressing sexuality needs in future ministerial and educational settings.

Sexually healthy religious professionals examine their own sexual attitudes and histories; are knowledgeable about sexuality, including sexual behaviors, sexual response, sexual orientation, gender identity, and personal relationships; have a commitment to gender and sexual justice; undertake periodic theological reflection on the integration of sexuality and spirituality; have the skills to provide pastoral care, worship, and referrals on sexuality issues; and are versed in their sacred texts, tradition's teachings and history, and denominational policies on sexuality issues.

Preparation of all students for ministry therefore must include:

- Required coursework on human sexuality and healthy professional boundaries.

- Regularly scheduled course offerings on sexuality issues, including courses on sexual ethics, LGBTQ theology, women in religious traditions and faith communities, and sexual abuse and domestic violence.

- Inclusion of sexuality topics in introductory and core courses, such as Hebrew Bible/Old Testament/Tanakh, New Testament, Theology/Systematics, Ethics, History, Midrash/Rabbinics/Code, Pastoral Counseling, Worship and Preaching, and Denomination-specific/polity classes.

- Required training for junior and senior faculty as well as deans and advisors on integrating sexuality issues into their classes, advising students with diverse sexualities, and maintaining appropriate professional boundaries.

In addition, a sexually healthy and responsible seminary has:

- A commitment to gender, racial/ethnic, and sexual diversity in its student body, faculty, staff, and leadership.

- Periodic worship opportunities that address sexuality issues.

- A commitment to inclusive language in worship and in the classroom.

- Library holdings that include current materials on sexuality and religion.

- Seminary-supported student groups that address sexual and gender identities and sexuality needs, such as a Women's Center, LGBTQ Group, Reproductive Rights Group, Support for Married/Coupled Seminarians, HIV Positive persons, and other sexuality-related groups.

- Anti-discrimination and full inclusion policies, addressing sex, race, disability, sexual orientation, gender identity, and marital status, that are widely included in catalogs, admission materials, faculty and student orientations, websites, and periodic postings in newsletters and announcements.

- A commitment to being safe from sexual harassment and abuse, including professional ethics and healthy boundaries policies for students, faculty, and staff and periodic required training opportunities.

- Faculty and leadership who are active on social and sexual justice issues in professional organizations, advocacy organizations, their denomination, and community, including research and publications, public witness, and activism.

The Religious Institute on Sexual Morality, Justice, and Healing sponsored a one-day colloquium on May 28, 2008 for leading seminary faculty, administrators, and sexuality educators. Participants who support this statement include Dr. Sarah (Sally) C. Conklin, Northern Illinois University; Rev. Dr. Marvin M. Ellison, Bangor Theological Seminary; Rev. Dr. Marie M. Fortune, FaithTrust Institute; Rev. Dr. Larry Greenfield, American Baptist Churches of Metro Chicago; Rev. Debra W. Haffner, Religious Institute on Sexual Morality, Justice, and Healing; Rev. Dr. Jay E. Johnson, Pacific School of Religion; Dr. Lori Lefkovitz, Reconstructionist Rabbinical College; Dr. Amy-Jill Levine, Vanderbilt University Divinity School; Dr. Su Yon Pak, Union Theological Seminary; Rabbi Mychal B. Springer, The Jewish Theological Seminary; and Rev. Dr. William Stayton, Widner University and Center for Sexuality and Religion.

Seminary Survey

The *Sex and the Seminary* survey evaluated the education and training in sexuality issues offered by seminaries. The results provide a current portrait of the state of sexuality education at leading seminaries and rabbinical schools in the U.S.

The survey was developed to assess an institution's performance in areas outlined in the Criteria for a Sexually Healthy and Responsible Seminary. To formally measure an institution's ability to meet the Criteria, the survey was divided into three major areas: Curricular, Institutional Environment, and Advocacy. In each of these areas, subcategories were developed to assess topical areas related to sexuality studies, LGBT/queer studies,[26] feminist/women's studies, and sexual abuse/violence studies.

1. **Curricular:** Questions focused on institutional offerings of degrees including majors, minors, and certificates, as well as course and learning opportunities including full-semester courses, introductory courses, and credit and non-credit workshops.

2. **Institutional Environment:** Questions assessed whether institutions have inclusion, anti-discrimination, inclusive language, and sexual harassment policy statements as well as how information regarding the policies is distributed; the demographics of faculty, staff, and students; worship service topics; and library holdings.

3. **Advocacy:** Questions addressed the degree of public involvement and commitment to issues of sexual justice by the president/dean and faculty, student

---

[26] LGBT is a commonly used acronym for Lesbian, Gay, Bisexual, and Transgender persons. LGBT studies are often identified as "Queer studies," however strictly speaking they are not the same field of study. Queer studies, as an academic discipline is grounded in queer theory. Carter Heyward writes, "Most queer theorists would find queer theology too mired in the politics of queer identity, just as most feminist liberation theologians find queer theory too apolitical to be very useful in this world in which surely even the stones cry out for justice. Still we are doing queer theology these days in seminary." See, Heyward, Carter (2003) "We're Here, We're Queer: Teaching Sex in Seminary," in *Body and Soul: Rethinking Sexuality as Justice Love*, eds. Marvin Ellison and Sylvia Thorson-Smith, (Pilgrim Press: Cleveland, OH), 78–96 for an historic, period-based description of the four movements of teaching sexuality in seminaries—feminist theology, theology of sexuality, sexual theology, and queer theology.

organizations and groups, and events hosted or sponsored by the institution.

Sample Selection. The seminaries were chosen to participate in the survey based on three criteria. First, faculty or leadership staff at the institution had endorsed the Religious Institute's Religious Declaration on Sexual Morality, Justice, and Healing. To that initial list, the advisory committee recommended additional institutions to provide geographic and religious diversity. In the end, fifty schools were identified as having at least some ongoing conversation regarding sexuality. The sample represents multiple faith traditions, sizes, geographic locations, and institutional affiliations. Thirty-six U.S. seminaries completed the survey, a 72% response rate. The list of participating institutions, their geographic location, and religious affiliation can be found on page 17.

Some institutions declined to participate. Three of the five Roman Catholic institutions did not respond to any communications. The remainder of the non-participants declined for one of the following reasons: insufficient time or staff resources to complete the survey, the topic was not an administrative priority, or they were undergoing a transition in leadership.

Each institution received an honorarium of $700.00 for participating in the survey. Half the stipend was paid upon receipt of a commitment form to participate and the other half after the full survey was completed. Each institution was also asked to select a lead person to take responsibility for completing the survey. The lead person served as the primary contact between the institution and the survey project director. The lead persons included administrative deans, staff, or faculty members.

Method. The survey focused primarily on the 2006–2007 academic year, but courses that were offered within a three-year period were permissible to include in order to provide a broader portrait of the participating institutions. Not every institution answered all 120 questions

as some questions depended on a positive answer to a previous question.

The survey was formatted through the online survey site Zoomerang.com. The Zoomerang tool provided a unique internet address for the study, so each school was able to enter its information directly. Each institution had to collect the data in advance of completing the online form.

Data Collection Challenges. Although the institutions surveyed are all seminaries that offer graduate-level training to religious professionals and clergy, there were many variations in institutional language, categorization, and even teaching structure. Questions needed to be sufficiently broad to address this diversity.

In addition, the length of the survey required diligence on the part of the lead person. Its depth and breadth often required consulting various institutional people and groups in order to confirm answers. Many of the survey coordinators described the survey as labor intensive. However, many also expressed interest in its results and said that they had learned a lot about their own institution's commitment to sexuality issues from participating.

Demographics. The institutions vary in size with the majority enrolling between 151 and 500 total students. On average, they have a slightly higher enrollment than the profile of Association of Theological Schools (ATS) accredited institutions in the U.S. Table 1 [page 16] compares the enrollment of ATS accredited schools to the enrollment of institutions in this survey.

Table 1: Institutional Size

Enrollment Size	ATS*	Sex and the Seminary Survey
Fewer than 75	10%	3%
75-150	26%	14%
151-300	30%	39%
301-500	17%	33%
501-1000	8%	11%
Over 1000	6%	

* US Institutions only.

The 36 seminaries represent a broad spectrum of denominational and institutional affiliations. A range of Protestant and Jewish seminaries or rabbinical schools are included as well as non-denominational and Unitarian Universalist (UUA) institutions. The survey sample is generally reflective of the denominational affiliation of most ATS institutions. Jewish Rabbinical schools are not members of ATS; their accrediting bodies are determined by regional higher education accreditation bodies. One Rabbinical school from each of the four major Jewish movements participated. Table 2 compares the denominational affiliations of ATS accredited schools with those of this study.

Participants also represent a variety of institutional structures, from independent and free-standing to departments within larger universities. The majority (25, 69%) of participants are associated with other institutions in some capacity, such as university affiliation (e.g.,

Candler School of Theology and Emory University) or a union of other theological schools (e.g., Episcopal Divinity School and the Union of Boston Theological Schools). Ten schools (28%) are associated only with a union or association of schools and fifteen (42%) are associated directly with a university. In comparison, ATS reports 34% of its institutions are university or college affiliated. They do not report the number of institutions that are affiliated with unions or associations of theological schools.

Does enrollment, denominational or institutional affiliation make a difference? The data is inconclusive, but does suggest a number of correlations. The seven institutions with a 151–300 level enrollment report having anti-discrimination and inclusion policies as well as LGBT/queer studies offerings at a higher rate than other institutions. Five of the seven institutions have a center devoted to sexuality-related issues and/or offer a major, minor, or certificate in sexuality-related areas. This combination of factors—size, having a center, and offering a degree in sexuality-related areas—generates an environment that meets a variety of the sexually healthy and responsible criteria and likely influences the seminary's programs and policies as well.

University-affiliated schools are least likely and unaffiliated schools are most likely to offer a skills-based course such as sexuality issues for religious professionals. Unaffiliated schools also offer worship and preaching courses on sexuality-related issues more often than

Table 2: Denominational Affiliation 2006-2007

ATS	Survey Sample		
57%	56% (20)	Protestant	Methodist (5), Presbyterian (4), Lutheran-ELCA United Church of Christ (3), Episcopal (2), American Baptist, Cooperative Baptist Fellowship, Christian Church [Disciples of Christ] (1)
21%	25% (9)	Non-Denominational	
	11% (4)	Jewish	Conservative (1), Orthodox (1), Reconstructionist (1), and Reform (1)
~1%	5% (2)	Unitarian Universalist Association	
22%	3% (1)	Roman Catholic	

Participating Institutions	Institution	State	Religious Affiliation
	Andover Newton Theological School	MA	United Church of Christ
	Bangor Theological Seminary	ME	United Church of Christ
	Brite Divinity School	TX	Christian Church (Disciples of Christ)
	Candler School of Theology, Emory University	GA	United Methodist
	Chicago Theological Seminary	IL	United Church of Christ
	Claremont School of Theology	CA	United Methodist
	Colgate Rochester/Crozier Divinity School	NY	American Baptist
	Columbia Theological Seminary	GA	Presbyterian Church (U.S.A.)
	Drew Theological School, Drew University	NJ	United Methodist
	Episcopal Divinity School	MA	Episcopal
	Garrett Evangelical Theological Seminary	IL	United Methodist
	General Theological Seminary	NY	Episcopal
	Harvard Divinity School	MA	Inter/nondenominational
	Hebrew Union College/Jewish Institute of Religion, Rabbinic School	NY	Reform Judaism
	Howard University School of Divinity	DC	Inter/nondenominational
	Interdenominational Theological Center (ITC)	GA	Inter/nondenominational
	Institute for Pastoral Studies, Loyola University of Chicago	IL	Roman Catholic
	The Jewish Theological Seminary	NY	Conservative Judaism
	Lutheran Theological Seminary (Gettysburg, PA)	PA	Evangelical Lutheran Church in America
	Mcafee School of Theology, Mercer University	GA	Cooperative Baptist Fellowship
	McCormick Theological Seminary	IL	Presbyterian Church (U.S.A.)
	Meadville Lombard Theological School	IL	Unitarian Universalist
	Pacific Lutheran Theological Seminary	CA	Evangelical Lutheran Church in America
	Pacific School of Religion	CA	Inter/nondenominational
	Princeton Theological Seminary	NJ	Presbyterian Church (U.S.A.)
	Reconstructionist Rabbinical College	PA	Reconstructionist Judaism
	San Francisco Theological Seminary	CA	Presbyterian Church (U.S.A.)
	Starr King School for the Ministry	CA	Unitarian Universalist
	Trinity Lutheran Seminary	OH	Evangelical Lutheran Church in America
	Union Theological Seminary (NYC)	NY	Inter/nondenominational
	United Theological Seminary	OH	United Methodist
	University of Chicago Divinity School	IL	Inter/nondenominational
	Vanderbilt University Divinity School	TN	Inter/nondenominational
	Wake Forest University School of Divinity	NC	Inter/nondenominational
	Yale University Divinity School	CT	Inter/nondenominational
	Yeshivat Chovevei Torah Rabbinical School	NY	Orthodox Judaism

other institutions. These results suggest a difference in how schools may approach their mission of training for ministry. University-affiliated institutions tend to offer more academic opportunities, while smaller, unaffiliated institutions focus more often on the professional training aspects of ministry.

Non/Inter-denominational affiliation affects offerings more than any individual religious affiliation. Non/Inter-denominational institutions are more likely to offer a major and slightly more likely to offer a minor or certificate in a sexuality-related area.

Sexuality Education in the Curriculum

Institutions were surveyed regarding their degree offerings for majors, minors, and certificates as well as their full-semester courses, introductory courses, and credit and non-credit workshops. The sexuality-related areas were divided into Sexuality-Related Issues for Religious Professionals, Women/Feminist Studies,[27] Sexual Ethics, LGBT/Queer Studies, and Sexual Abuse/Domestic Violence. Recognizing that many Master's level programs have a three-year rotation for non-introductory, full-semester courses, respondents were asked the frequency of course offerings.

Survey answers also recorded instructor's rank, course size, and whether the course was required for graduation or for a major. In the case of introductory courses and other learning opportunities, the survey sought to determine which sexuality topics are addressed routinely across the curriculum. A positive response to these course offerings and to topic areas covered was reported by the lead person at the institution. The survey did not ask about course methodology or content. The Religious Institute also did not verify information about which topics were covered with the individual faculty member.

Degree Offerings

Each institution surveyed offers a Master of Divinity or its equivalent (36, 100%), while most offer a Masters of Arts (26, 72%). Other degree offerings include a Doctorate in Ministry (20, 56%), Masters in Theology (12, 33%), and a Masters of Sacred Theology (8, 22%). Several institutions also offer a Doctorate of Philosophy or Theology (7, 19%).

Twenty-four institutions (66%) offer the opportunity for Master's level students to specialize in a non-traditional area outside of the usual fields of scripture/bible, theology, history, ethics, and pastoral care.

Almost two-thirds (15 of 24, 62%) of the institutions with non-traditional majors, minors, or certificates offer a specialization in sexuality, women/feminist, or LGBT/queer studies.

- Thirteen institutions (54%) offer a women/feminist studies major, minor, or certificate.
- Four institutions (17%) offer a sexuality studies major, minor, or certificate.
- Four institutions (17%) offer an LGBT/queer studies major, minor, or certificate.

Four institutions offer more than one sexuality-related specialization. For example, one institution offers a major in both sexuality and LGBT/queer studies. Institutions which offer LGBT/queer studies or sexuality as a major, minor, or certificate are more likely to meet a range of the sexually healthy and responsible criteria including coverage of sexuality-related issues in course offerings, worship experiences, policies for inclusion and anti-discrimination, student groups, and advocacy on the part of faculty and administrators.

---

[27] Women/feminist studies courses include any course specifically addressing women or feminist theory/practices in the disciplines of scripture, ethics, theology, counseling, or ministry. Courses that fit into this area include, for example, Women's Ways of Preaching, Women in the New Testament, or Womanist and Feminist Ethics.

Full-Semester Courses

Full-semester course offerings provide a seminary student with the most sustained and in-depth educational opportunity for coursework. The survey studied full-semester course offerings in the following fields:

- Women/feminist studies
- LGBT/queer studies
- Sexual abuse/domestic violence
- Sexual ethics
- Sexuality issues for religious professionals

Most institutions (31, 86%) report offering a regularly scheduled, full-semester course in an area of women/feminist studies. The number of schools offering full-semester courses in other sexuality-related topic areas drops significantly. Just over half (20, 56%) offer a course in sexual ethics. One-third of the institutions offer courses on sexual abuse and domestic violence and sexuality issues for religious professionals. Only ten (28%) offer a full-semester course devoted explicitly to LGBT/queer studies.

Additional data on full-semester courses reveals a gap in upcoming tenure-track faculty providing sexuality courses. Institutions reported that sexuality-related full-semester courses are offered primarily by senior professors (50–70% of the time) and adjunct/lecturers (30–50% of the time). Conversely, LGBT/queer studies courses are more likely to be taught by adjunct/lecturers (60%) than by senior professors (40%).

Sexuality-related courses are taught infrequently. Seventy percent of the full-semester courses are only taught every two to three years. Only three institutions (8%) teach LGBT/queer studies every year; only three teach sexuality issues for religious professionals annually; and, only three teach a sexual abuse/domestic violence course every year. Six institutions (17%) teach a sexual ethics course each year and eleven institutions (31%) teach a women/feminist studies course each year.

The vast majority of schools do not require these courses for graduation.

- Only one institution (3%) requires a full-semester course on sexuality issues for religious professionals for graduation.
- Only two (6%) require a full-semester course in LGBT/queer studies.
- Only three (8%) require a full-semester course on sexual abuse and domestic violence.
- Only six (17%) require a full-semester course on sexual ethics.
- Only six (17%) require a full-semester course in women/feminist studies.

Table 3 provides information on the institutions offering a full-semester course, graduation requirement, frequency of offering, and whether or not the offering is an elective. The box on page 20 provides an alternative portrait of the classes by subject area.

Table 3: Full Semester Courses

Enrollment Size	Total Institutions	Require Course for Graduation	Offered at least Once a Year	Course Offered as an Elective
Women/Feminist Studies	31 (86%)	6 (17%)	11 (31%)	25 (69%)
Sexual Ethics	20 (58%)	6 (17%)	6 (17%)	11 (31%)
Sexual Abuse and Domestic Violence	12 (33%)	3 (8%)	3 (8%)	9 (25%)
Sexuality Issues for Religious Professionals	12 (33%)	1 (3%)	3 (8%)	10 (28%)
GLBT/Queer Studies	10 (28%)	2 (6%)	3 (8%)	7 (19%)

Full Semester Course Information

LGBT/Queer Studies in Religion. Ten (28%) institutions report a full-semester course on LGBT/queer studies in religion. Seven of these schools offer this course once every two to three years. At five schools, the course is taught by non-full time faculty, such as a lecturer or adjunct; at four, by senior professors; and at one by a permanent, non-tenure track instructor. Six percent of schools (2) require the course for graduation, 6% (2) require it for a field specialization, and 19% (7) report it as an elective.

Sexuality-Related Issues for Ministry. Twelve institutions (33%) offer a full-semester course on sexuality-related issues for ministry. Only three (8%) offer the course every semester or every year. It is taught half the time by senior professors and half by adjunct/lecturers. Only one institution requires it for graduation.

Sexual Abuse and Domestic Violence. One-third (12) of institutions offer a full-semester course on sexual abuse and domestic violence. Nine of these schools offer the course on a two-to-three-year rotation. Seven offer this course in the area of Pastoral Care. Senior professors (50%) and junior professors (17%) teach over half (8) of the courses. Only eight percent (3) of all schools require this course for graduation.

Sexual Ethics. Just over half of all reporting institutions offer a full-semester course on sexual ethics. Most of these (14 of 20, 70%) seminaries offer the course on a two-to-three-year rotation. This course is taught by the highest percentage of senior professors (65%) and an additional 5% by junior professors. Seventeen percent of institutions require the course for graduation, eleven percent require it for a field specialization, and thirty-one percent report it as an elective.

Women/Feminist Studies in Religion. Sixty-five percent of courses under the umbrella category of women and religion—including theology, scripture, ethics, history, and ministry—are offered on the two-to-three-year cycle and forty percent are taught by senior faculty. Seventeen percent (6) of these courses are required for graduation and eleven percent (4) report the courses are required for a field specialization.

Introductory Courses

Introductory courses reach the largest student audience and are required by most seminaries. Participating institutions were asked whether certain topics were covered in one class period or woven throughout the course. Topics include the role of women, LGBT issues, sexual violence, sexuality and spirituality, sexuality, gender,[28] and reproduction/family. Overall, the role of women and gender are consistently covered in higher percentages across the curriculum than any other topics in the survey. The role of women is covered on average 70% of the time across introductory courses; gender is covered on average 67% of the time.

Many sexuality-related topics are covered in most introductory courses. However, only ten schools address sexuality-related topics in a single class period in all relevant introductory courses.[29] Sexuality-related topics are covered most often in introductory courses in Pastoral

---

[28] Gender is "an individual's personal, social and/or legal status as female, male or transgender. Words that describe gender include 'feminine,' 'masculine' and 'transgender.' Gender is a cultural construct that reflects a society's expectations for feminine and masculine qualities and behaviors." Gender in the context of these responses most likely reflects discussion of the social construction of masculinity and femininity, not coverage of transgender issues. See Timothy Palmer, et al. (2007) *A Time to Seek: Study Guide on Sexual and Gender Diversity,* Westport, CT: Religious Institute on Sexual Morality, Justice, and Healing.
[29] Institutions were not counted in areas in which they do not offer introductory courses, e.g., in the category of New Testament, Jewish institutions were not part of the total institutions number.

Care and Practical Theology. Introductory courses cover women in religion and gender two to four times as often as sexuality or LGBT/queer areas of study. Sexuality is on average covered more often than LGBT issues. However, in worship and/or preaching, ethics, and polity/denominational courses, LGBT issues are covered more often than sexuality. (Table 4)

Workshops

Workshop offerings, both credit and non-credit, supplement the course-based curriculum. Institutions were asked about workshop offerings in the same topic areas as full-semester courses as well as sexual harassment prevention. Workshops are often fewer hours and lack the depth of a full-semester course. Some institutions offer either a workshop or a full course on these topics, some offer both, and some offer neither. The categories of work-shops and full-semester courses were combined to reflect the learning opportunities supported by the institution.

Seminaries offer women/feminist studies learning opportunities most often (89%), followed closely by sexual harassment prevention (81%), sexual ethics (75%), sexual abuse and domestic violence (69%), and sexuality issues for religious professionals (69%). LGBT/queer studies learning opportunities are offered by only one third of the seminaries (36%).

Sexual harassment prevention learning opportunities are offered by 81% (29) of institutions. While rarely a full course offering, it is the topic that is most often covered through alternative learning opportunities (25, 69%). Unlike other sexuality components, a majority of schools assure that their graduates have a sexual harassment

Table 4: **Introductory Courses - Topical Coverage**

Role of Women   Gender
Sexuality   LGBT Issues

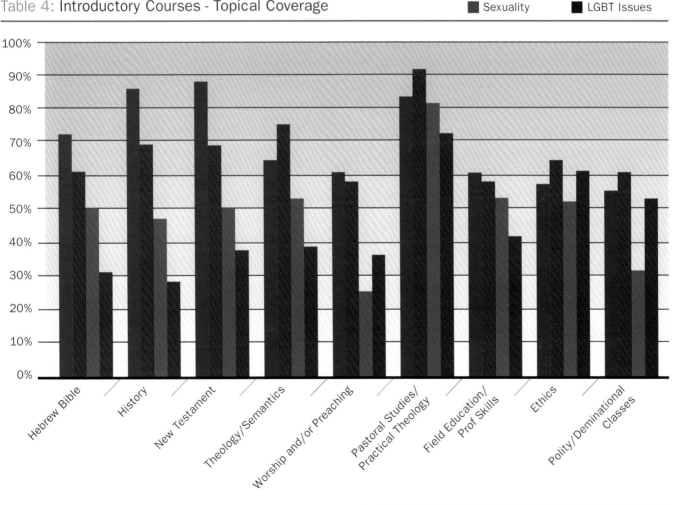

Table 5: Learning Opportunities

	Women/ Feminist Studies	Sexual Ethics	Sexual Abuse & Domestic Violence	Sexual Harassment Prevention	Sexuality Issues for Religious Professionals	GLBT/ Queer Studies
Full Semester Course	31	20	12	4	11	10
Credit/Non-credit Workshop	20	16	20	25	17	9
Total Schools	32	27	25	29	25	13
% of Total Schools	89%	75%	69%	81%	69%	36%

offering. Sixty-seven percent (24) of institutions require a class or workshop for ministry students and thirty-nine percent (14) require it of all students. Table 5 presents the number of institutions offering full-semester courses and credit/non-credit workshops in the major sexuality-related course areas.

Institutional Commitment to Sexuality-Related Issues

A sexually healthy and responsible seminary supports a commitment to gender, racial/ethnic, and sexual diversity, through policies, worship, library holdings, and the composition by gender of administrators and faculty. While the explicit curriculum of a seminary includes structured courses and workshops, its implicit curriculum includes how the administration addresses, and the environment supports, sexuality-related issues. A number of institutions have a center or institute dedicated specifically to sexuality-related issues that influences the overall environment.[30]

Policies

Policies provide one of the most concrete measures of institutional support. They serve as an institution's commitment to sexual diversities. Some policies exist to comply with state and/or federal anti-discrimination law; in contrast, inclusion policies demonstrate an overt commitment to, and welcoming of, diverse individuals.

Anti-discrimination. As required by federal law, written anti-discrimination policies on the basis of sex are in place at all 36 schools. Thirty-two (89%) have a written anti-discrimination policy on the basis of sexual orientation, and 21 (58%) include gender identity (transgender) in these policies. Two institutions are in the process of modifying their policies to include gender identity. (Table 6)

Table 6: Anti-Discrimination Policies

Anti-discrimination Policies for:		
Sex	36	100%
Sexual Orientation	32	89%
Gender Identity	21	58%

Inclusion. Many anti-discrimination policies are required by federal and/or state law. Inclusion policies are voluntary measures to encourage and welcome diversity in an institution. There are significantly fewer inclusion polices than anti-discrimination policies. More than half of the institutions reported written policies in place on the full inclusion of women (20, 56%) and exactly half on gay and lesbian persons (18, 50%). Forty-four percent of schools have written policies requiring full inclusion of bisexual persons (16) and 39% have policies on transgender persons (14). Nine (25%) institutions do not have any written inclusion policies. (Table 7)

Sexual harassment. Few institutions had policies on sexual harassment thirty years ago. Now almost all do.

---

[30] A brief description of the centers is on page 30 in the section on model seminary practices.

Table 7: Full Inclusion Policies

Full-Inclusion Policies for:		
Women	20	56%
Gay & Lesbian Persons	18	50%
Bisexual Persons	16	44%
Transgender Persons	14	39%
None of the Above	9	25%

Ninety-seven percent (35) of surveyed institutions have sexual harassment policies for intra-faculty/staff relationships and faculty/staff-to-student relationships. Eighty-nine percent (32) of institutions have written policies governing student-to-student relationships. Institutions reported that policies include how to handle complaints. (Table 8) Most often, policies are communicated to the seminary community in writing via catalogues, bulletins, student/staff handbooks, and admissions materials. The information is most frequently discussed or handed out at orientation, posted in public spaces on bulletin boards and occasionally on an institution's website.

Table 8: Sexual Harassment Policies

Policies for Sexual Harassment for:		
Intra-Faculty/Staff	35	97%
Faculty/Staff-to-Student	35	97%
Student-to-Student	32	89%

Inclusive language. Inclusive language policies call for language that encompasses diverse genders and sexes in order to affirm the diversity of people. At seminaries, policies may require inclusive references to God as well. Twenty-nine institutions (81%) have some type of inclusion policy. Fourteen (39%) institutions report having a written policy mandating use of inclusive language in classrooms and worship. An additional fifteen (42%) institutions have an inclusive language policy specifically for worship.

Worship

Most seminaries conduct worship services throughout the year. Over half of the institutions surveyed report

conducting one or more worship services on a sexuality issue within the past year (21, 58%). LGBT concerns are covered more frequently than any other topic in worship services on sexuality issues. Worship represents one of the few categories where LGBT issues are more prevalent than women in religion/feminist studies.

Worship services focused most often on LGB experiences (47%); close to half of the LGB worship services also included transgender experiences (19%). Only one in five institutions addressed sexuality in general (19%), and fewer than one in six held worship services that focused on reproductive health and rights (14%). Only three (8%) covered sexual violence and domestic abuse. (Table 9)

Table 9: Worship Services

The worship service(s) focused on:		
Gay, Lesbian, & Bisexual Experiences	17	47%
Women in Religion	16	44%
HIV/AIDS	12	33%
Sexuality	7	19%
Transgender Experiences	7	19%
Reproductive Health/Rights	5	14%
Sexual Violence/Domestic Abuse	3	8%

Library Holdings

Library holdings demonstrate a commitment to providing campus resources on sexuality-related issues. Books, journals, and curricula complement student and faculty research, worship development, and course content. Almost all institutions (94%) report their library has more than ten books published since 2000 on topics of sexuality and religion. Seventy-five percent said they have journals that specifically address a cross-section of sexuality and religion. Library journal subscriptions include the *Journal of Feminist Studies in Religion* (85%), *Theology & Sexuality* (76%), and *Journal of Women and Religion* (73%). Half (53%) have curricula on sexuality education from denominations or independent presses in their holdings. Only two institutions (6%) said their library had none of these resources.

Institutional Leadership

Institutions reported the sex of their students, administration, faculty, and board of trustees.[31] While the survey suggests a commitment to women/feminist and gender issues in courses, women's centers, student advocacy/caucus groups, and anti-discrimination and inclusion policies, the presence of women as participants in the seminary environment is only balanced in the student body. There is still a stained glass ceiling for women faculty, administrators, and boards of trustees. Two-thirds of institutions do not have gender parity in their faculty, administration, and boards. Only one-third had women in senior leadership and only 10 seminaries had gender balance on their board of trustees. (Table 10)

Women's presence in leadership makes a difference in the overall sexual health of the seminary. When women represent at least 40% of the faculty, institutions are more likely to offer full-semester courses in women/feminist studies, sexual ethics, LGBT/queer studies, sexuality issues for religious professionals, and sexual abuse/domestic violence. Two institutions reported one student who identifies as

Table 10: Institutional Leadership

More than 40% Women:				
	Students	Faculty	Senior Leadership	Board of Trustees
#	35	14	13	10
%	97%	39%	36%	28%

---

[31] In the pilot study, legal and logistical concerns were raised about including questions on sexual orientation and racial/ethnic background. Therefore, the survey did not request demographic information on the racial/ethnic background or sexual orientation of students, faculty, administrators, or boards of trustees.

transgender and one also had a faculty member who identifies as transgender.

Advocacy and Support for Sexuality-Related Issues

Advocacy by its administration, faculty, and staff is a visible means for an institution to voice its priorities and goals to the wider community. Advocacy can take the form of news media contributions, published writings or commentary, participation on boards of sexual justice organizations, as well as on-campus events that further dialogue on sexuality-related topics. In addition, students may be offered support and educated in advocacy through participation in small groups and student organizations. These groups are generally initiated and run by students.

Public Voice

In the last year, one-third of the institutions (12, 33%) report that their president or dean was interviewed by a news media source on a sexual justice issue. Of those interviewed, three were women and nine were men. They most often discussed LGBT issues (83%), sexuality and spirituality (58%), sexual relationships (50%), and sexuality issues for professionals (50%).

Most schools (27, 75%) report that in the past two years, faculty members or senior administrative staff have published or have appeared in the media addressing a sexuality issue. Similar to presidents and deans, the most commonly addressed topic was LGBT issues (53%), followed by gender, sexuality, and spirituality. Other topics included sexual relationships, sexual abuse/domestic violence, HIV/AIDS, sexuality issues for professionals, reproductive health, and sexuality and pleasure. Fifteen (42%) institutions identified faculty members who participate on boards of sexual justice organizations.

Events

In the past two years, 25 (69%) institutions sponsored or co-sponsored events on sexual or reproductive justice issues. Events included outside speakers for an institution-wide event (50%), conferences on sexuality or sexual issues (33%), dramatic presentations such as a reading of *The Vagina Monologues* (19%), conferences on reproductive health/rights (14%), and organizing and providing transportation to an off-campus reproductive choice rally (3%).

Small Groups and Student Organizations

Student organizations and groups are initiated and facilitated primarily by students with faculty oversight. Most institutions (29, 81%) have small advocacy/identity student groups and organizations. At these schools, 75% (22) report groups for LGBT persons (e.g., Queer Caucus) and an equal number have women's groups (e.g., Women's Center). In contrast, only one-third report groups that support married/coupled seminarians (33%) and only a few institutions have groups on reproductive rights (21%) or for HIV-positive persons (10%). (Table 11)

Table 11: Small Group/Student Organizations

Group/Student Organization		Percentage of Institutions with Groups	Percentage of Total Schools
LGBT Persons (e.g. Queer Caucus)	22	75%	61%
Women (e.g. Women's Center)	22	75%	61%
Support for Married/Couple Seminarians	12	41%	33%
Reproductive Rights Group	6	21%	17%
HIV Positive Persons	3	10%	8%
We do not off or support such groups	7		19%

Model Seminary Practices

This portrait of what the seminaries are doing—and are not doing—demonstrates a clear need for improvement on sexuality-related issues across the curriculum, the institutional environment, and seminary faculty and leadership. In analyzing the findings, ten seminaries stood out. While even these institutions can improve in quality and scope, they offer models of seminaries that have made an institutional commitment to curricular offerings, policies, gender parity, and advocacy on sexuality-related issues.

The final step in the analysis of research was the development of an institutional profile for each seminary based on how it met the Criteria for a Sexually Healthy and Responsible Seminary. The categories balance institutionally sustained commitments such as policy or course requirements with institutional factors such as faculty demographics and student involvement in various advocacy groups or events.

The criteria assessed included:

Curricular Criteria
- Sexuality-related issues are covered in all relevant introductory courses.
- A full-semester course on sexuality issues for religious professionals and LGBT/queer studies is offered.
- These courses are required for graduation and taught at least once an academic year.
- The three other sexuality-related full-semester courses (women/feminist studies, sexual ethics, and sexual violence/domestic violence) are offered.
- A major, minor, or certificate in LGBT/queer or sexuality studies is offered.
- A learning opportunity on sexual harassment prevention or sexual abuse/domestic violence is offered and required for graduation.

Institutional Commitment Criteria

- The institution has a written policy on sexual harassment for faculty-to-student relationships, intra-faculty/staff, and/or student-to-student relationships.
- The institution has a written policy against discrimination on the basis of sex, sexual orientation, and/or gender identity.
- The institution has a written policy on full inclusion of gay/lesbian, bisexual, transgender, and/or women.
- Women comprise at least 40% of students, faculty, senior leadership, and/or board of trustees

Advocacy Criteria

- The institution has held a worship service to address a sexuality-related topic in the past year.
- Faculty members engage in public advocacy through publishing, media appearances, or leadership in sexuality-related organizations.
- The institution has held an event on campus related to sexuality issues.

Leading Institutions

The results of the survey suggest that even the most committed seminaries have room to improve their curricular offerings, policies, and ministerial training requirements. No one institution meets all the criteria, thus each of the seminaries studied showed room for improvement in adequately addressing sexuality-related needs.

Ten seminaries (28%) meet at least two-thirds of the criteria. They are listed in the box (right). Fifteen seminaries (42%) meet less than half of the criteria.

When broken down by type of criteria—curricular, institutional, and advocacy—trends are visible in what seminaries are doing and where improvements could be made. Table 12 on page 28 presents the percentage of seminaries meeting the individual criteria. Overall, policies on

Leading Institutions

Andover Newton Theological School

Candler School of Theology

Chicago Theological Seminary

Claremont School of Theology

Drew Theological School

Episcopal Divinity School

Harvard Divinity School

Reconstructionist Rabbinical College

Vanderbilt University Divinity School

Wake Forest University Divinity School

sexual harassment, anti-discrimination and offerings for sexual harassment prevention are currently supported by the vast majority of seminaries. Student bodies reflect gender parity, and many seminaries engage in advocacy on sexuality-related issues. Yet, most institutions need to improve in the areas of course offerings, inclusion policies, worship opportunities, and gender parity of faculty, administration, and board composition (Table 12, see page 28).

Centers

In the survey, nine institutions (25%) reported having a free-standing center, program, or institute that deals directly with sexuality-related issues including sexuality issues in ministry, LGBT/queer studies, and women/feminist studies. (While the focus and structure of the centers, programs and institutes varies, for clarity, we refer to them collectively as centers.) Most centers provide training for clergy, students, and faculty; this training is most often for students (6, 66%) and continuing education for alumni (5, 55%). Almost half (4, 45%) focus primarily on academic research initiatives.

Religious Institute staff conducted phone and e-mail interviews with staff at each of the centers. Interviews

Table 12: Criteria for Model Practices

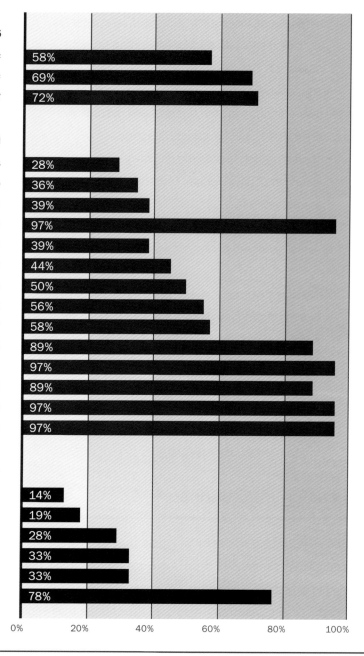

Advocacy Criteria for Model Seminaries

Held Worship on sexually related Topic	58%
Institutions who held an Event on sexuality related Topic	69%
Institutions where Faculty engage in Public Advocacy	72%

Institutional Commitment Criteria

Institutions with more than 40% Women on Board of Trustees	28%
Institutions with more than 40% Women in Senior Leadership	36%
Institutions with more than 40% Women on the Faculty	39%
Institutions with more than 40% Women Students	97%
Full Inclusion Policy for Transgender Persons	39%
Full Inclusion Policy for Bisexual Persons	44%
Full Inclusion Policy for Gay Men and Lesbians	50%
Full Inclusion Policy for Women	56%
Anti-Discrimination Policy on the basis of Gender	58%
Anti-Discrimination Policy on the basis of Sexual Orientation	89%
Anti-Discrimination Policy on the basis of Sex	97%
Sexual Harassment Policy for Student-to-Student Relationship	89%
Sexual Harassment Policy for Faculty/Staff-to-Student Relationships	97%
Sexual Harassment Policy for intra-Faculty/Staff Relationships	97%

Curricular Criteria for Model Seminaries

Has a Major, Minor, or Certificate in Sexuality or LGBT/Queer Studies	14%
Offers the three other full semester Courses	19%
Offer LGBT/Queer Studies - full semester Course	28%
Offer Sexuality Issue for Religious Professionals	33%
Cover Sex related issues in all relevant intro Courses	33%
Offer a learning Opportunity in Sexual Harassment	78%

with directors or staff of the centers suggest that most centers began out of a realization that particular under-represented sexuality issues or groups (e.g., women's and LGBT equality) were not being addressed by the seminary. Most interviewees expressed an institutionally supportive culture as part of their success. Some suggested that this may not have been the case during the initial development and growth of the centers, but it is true now that they are established. Center directors and staff noted that although they focus on sexuality-related issues, they also promote research and programming that is attentive to the intersection of social justice issues such as racism, poverty, globalization, and inter-religious dialogue.

Centers, programs, and institutes have a positive impact on the overall sexual health of the seminary. Six of the nine institutions (66%) which have a center dedicated to sexuality issues meet at least 60% of the criteria for a sexually healthy and responsible seminary. For a brief description of each, see pages 30-31.

The institutional impact of the centers results in increased course offerings, workshops, and learning opportunities in sexuality-related topics; faculty positions with a specialization in sexuality-related research; and often greater advocacy on sexuality-related issues. While most are staffed by full-time faculty (6, 66%) and students (7, 78%), about half have full-time administrative staff (4, 44%). The majority of centers are supported by grant funding or endowed gift (7, 78%).

The major contributions of a center to the sexual health of a seminary include:

1. Increased curricular offerings on sexuality issues: Free-standing centers provide additional programming and staff that increase the variety of educational opportunities a seminary has the capacity to provide. Curricular offerings may include hosting workshops for credit or non-credit, bringing visiting faculty, and/or creating a new position for faculty with specialization in sexuality-related areas. In four of the eight programs, a certificate in a sexuality-related area is offered by the center, which supports the certificate requirements with faculty to teach courses and serve as advisors.

2. Demonstrated public commitment to sexuality issues: Center staff serve as advocates for the importance of sexuality issues in the seminary context. A number of interviewees remarked that the centers were a safe space for students looking to organize around important sexuality-related issues. This public commitment also generally extends beyond the institutional walls to public witness to religious congregations and denominations or society at large through educational training, media appearances, or hosting of events.

3. Improved sexuality-related resources: Many of the centers produce and collect resources regarding their particular sexuality-related focus. For example, some of the centers have syllabus collections or bibliographies for research and teaching use. Others record rituals and worship services.

Many host colloquia generating new research and providing space for important and innovative conversations. These resources are available to alumni, area clergy, and students.

Faculty and Courses

There are a variety of sexuality courses being taught in the institutions surveyed. However, as discussed on page 19, only one in ten institutions requires students to take such courses. Institutional commitment to offering sexuality-related courses is influenced by course requirements for graduation or concentration, and the presence of faculty with a specialization in sexuality-related fields. In addition to the data collected from the original survey, the Religious Institute conducted a follow-up faculty survey as well as a review of sexuality-related course syllabi.

The follow-up survey was completed by faculty who were identified by the seminary as teaching a full-semester course on sexuality issues for religious professionals or LGBT/queer studies. Only faculty members who had volunteered to share their contact information in the first phase of the survey were contacted. The syllabi collection and review included contacting faculty teaching any of the sexuality-related full-semester courses. Some faculty provided more than one syllabus.

Faculty Survey

The Religious Institute staff also conducted a follow-up written survey with 14 faculty members. Fourteen of eighteen (78%) invited faculty completed the survey. Eight of the courses reported focus on sexuality issues for religious professionals and seven on LGBT/queer studies. One faculty member taught both courses. The courses are primarily taught once every two to three years (73%) with an average student enrollment of 10–20 students (79%). None of the courses were required for graduation.

These two types of courses tend to be interdisciplinary and cover a range of topics. When comparing the courses, the most likely area to be addressed is Scripture (100%).

Sexuality-Related Centers at Seminaries

The **Carpenter Program in Religion, Gender, and Sexuality** at Vanderbilt University Divinity School was started in 1996 to foster conversation about religion, gender, and sexuality. The program seeks to provide education through events, course offerings, and conferences as a way to "encourage communication within and across religious affiliations, ideological bases, and cultural contexts." The program administers a certificate in Religion, Gender, and Sexuality.

http://www.vanderbilt.edu/divinity/carpenter/

The **Center for Lesbian and Gay Studies in Religion and Ministry (CLGS)** at the Pacific School of Religion was started in 2000 to "advance the well-being of the LGBT community and to transform faith communities and the wider society by taking a leading role in shaping a new public discourse on religion and sexuality through education, creative scholarship, research, community building, advocacy, and presenting a new public voice in the debate over sexual identity through media outreach and coalition building." The center provides courses, events, on-line resources, and training. The center also offers a certificate in Sexuality and Religion.

http://www.clgs.org/

The **Center for Sexuality and Christian Life (CSCL)** at the Claremont School of Theology was established to "foster intellectual inquiry and open dialogue within the Church and other interested religious communities on the complex issue of human sexuality and seeks to prepare leaders to know and understand human sexuality and the ways that it is important in the Church, the academy, and the world." The center maintains a collection of sexuality-based resources. CSCL began in the early 1990s, but was reconstituted in 2004 as a forum for discussing issues of sexuality particular to the Methodist tradition, but also within the wider Christian community through gatherings at the seminary and advocacy work within communities.

http://www.cst.edu/current_students/cscl.php

The **Institute for Judaism & Sexual Orientation (IJSO)** at Hebrew Union College-Jewish Institute of Religion (HUC-JIR) provides Jewish leadership to "change congregational attitudes and policies toward inclusion of each and every Jew, regardless of sexual orientation or gender identity among the organizational arms of the Reform Movement." IJSO was established in 2005 and has become an online resource for all four Hebrew Union College campuses including a web-based learning site, events, and resources for translation, ritual, and worship.

http://elearning.huc.edu/jhvrc/

Isha El Akhota: The Women's Center at the Jewish Theological Seminary was founded to support the religious, academic, and professional needs of JTS's diverse women's community. When JTS began admitting female Rabbinical students in 1984, students created the center, which was later endowed, allowing for a space and programming. With the 2007 admission of Lesbian and Gay students to the Rabbinical school, the center has broadened its programming and advocacy efforts to include sexual orientation and identity issues.

http://www.jtsa.edu/x1701.xml

Kolot: The Center for Jewish Women's & Gender Studies at the Reconstructionist Rabbinical College started 12 years ago to "bring insight and innovative practices from the study of gender and Judaism to the Jewish community, in addition to offering courses, pastoral education, and faculty education." The center runs a certificate program in Jewish Women's Studies with Temple University. The center provides a variety of online resources including a syllabi collection and ritual and ceremonies website (http://www.ritualwell.org).
http://www.kolot.org

The **LGBTQ Religious Studies Center** at Chicago Theological Seminary was founded in 2006 as a "theological think tank and a resource for activists." It houses the Lesbian, Gay, Bisexual and Transgender (LGBT) Religious Archives Network (began by CTS in 2002), a resource for students and researchers studying the history of LGBT religious movements (http://www.lgbtran.org/). The center explores "critical issues in theology and ethics from a LGBTQ perspective" including support of new faculty scholarship, hosting events, promoting religious voices in the media, and curricular evaluation. The center supports a Certificate in Theological Education with a Concentration in LGBTQ studies.
http://www.ctschicago.edu/academic/LGBTQ.php

Women IMAGES (Women in Ministry at Garrett-Evangelical Seminary) at Garrett-Evangelical Theological Seminary was founded in the late 1970s to provide "community and educational opportunities for women and seeks to create a nonsexist context for theological education." The center has been influential in articulating a need for women faculty and curricular change to address a variety of women's issues.
http://www.garrett.edu/content.asp?A=5&C=20158

The **Women's Studies in Religion Program (WSRP)** at Harvard Divinity School began in 1973. WSRP promotes "critical inquiry into the interaction between religion and gender. It sponsors research and teaching in feminist theology biblical studies, ethics, and women's history, as well as interdisciplinary scholarship on women throughout the world's religions." The program annually supports five visiting research associates in the development of new primary research. That research is dispersed through courses, publications, and events. The Women, Gender, Sexuality and Religion degree focus at Harvard Divinity School is not directly supported by the center, but its courses and events complement the offering.
http://www.hds.harvard.edu/wsrp/

*All quotations are taken from centers' websites.

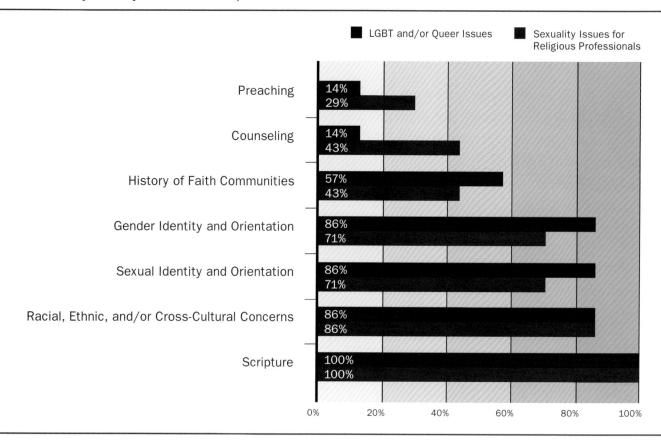

■ LGBT and/or Queer Issues   ■ Sexuality Issues for Religious Professionals

Preaching — 14% / 29%
Counseling — 14% / 43%
History of Faith Communities — 57% / 43%
Gender Identity and Orientation — 86% / 71%
Sexual Identity and Orientation — 86% / 71%
Racial, Ethnic, and/or Cross-Cultural Concerns — 86% / 86%
Scripture — 100% / 100%

Racial, ethnic and/or cross-cultural concerns, sexual identity and orientation, gender identity and orientation, and history of faith communities are covered equally or more often in LGBT/queer studies courses. Preaching and counseling are covered more often in sexuality issues for religious professionals courses. (Table 13)

LGBT/queer studies courses covered Scripture and theology most often (100%). Ethics, gender identity and orientation, racial ethnic and/or cross-cultural concerns, sexual identity and orientation, sexuality-related spiritual practices, and transgender concerns are covered by 85% of the courses. Bisexual, lesbian, and gay male issues follow closely in 70% of courses. Over half the courses cover history of faith communities, liturgy, and the science of sexuality. Skills related to preaching and counseling are addressed least often (14%). (Table 14)

Sexuality issues for religious professionals courses cover Scripture (100%), racial, ethnic and or/cross-cultural

concerns (86%), as well as sexual and gender diversity issues (71%). Attraction and boundaries are covered in over two-thirds of courses. Less than half of the courses (43%) cover counseling, history of faith communities, sex abuse prevention, sexual behaviors and response, sexual development, and sexuality education. Foundational issues and ministry-related issues such as preaching and anatomy and physiology are covered in one-third of classes. (Table 15)

Most faculty reported that their course does not cover all of the sexuality issues and that students needed further training. Faculty most often noted the need for follow-up training for students in clergy misconduct, violence and abuse issues, and sexuality education.

Faculty listed a number of ways that they received their own training to teach sexuality-related courses. While all have a doctorate degree in their discipline, many reported a need for further training which they sought

Table 14: LGBT/Queer Studies Courses

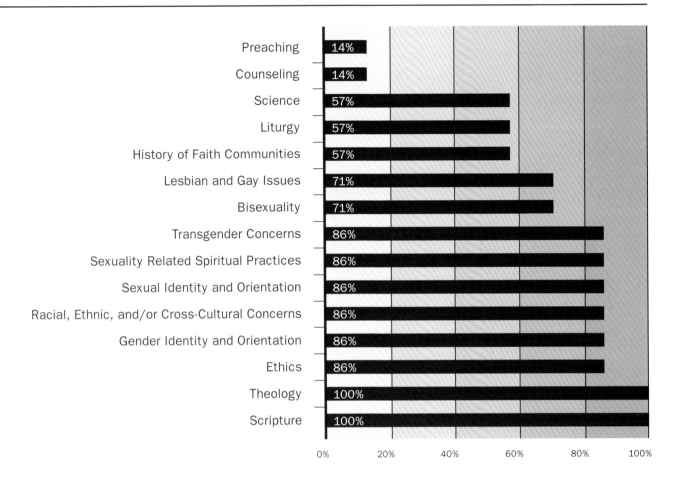

Category	Percentage
Preaching	14%
Counseling	14%
Science	57%
Liturgy	57%
History of Faith Communities	57%
Lesbian and Gay Issues	71%
Bisexuality	71%
Transgender Concerns	86%
Sexuality Related Spiritual Practices	86%
Sexual Identity and Orientation	86%
Racial, Ethnic, and/or Cross-Cultural Concerns	86%
Gender Identity and Orientation	86%
Ethics	86%
Theology	100%
Scripture	100%

Table 15: Sexuality Issues for Religious Professionals Course Content

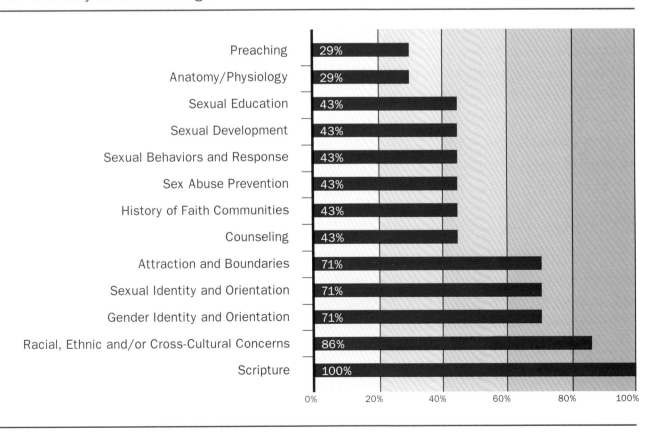

Category	Percentage
Preaching	29%
Anatomy/Physiology	29%
Sexual Education	43%
Sexual Development	43%
Sexual Behaviors and Response	43%
Sex Abuse Prevention	43%
History of Faith Communities	43%
Counseling	43%
Attraction and Boundaries	71%
Sexual Identity and Orientation	71%
Gender Identity and Orientation	71%
Racial, Ethnic and/or Cross-Cultural Concerns	86%
Scripture	100%

through sexual and reproductive health groups, pastoral work with specific populations (LGBT community, women in shelters, abortion providers), and counseling training. Faculty reported that further training, network building, and resource sharing would assist them in further developing their sexuality-related courses.

Syllabus Review

The review of syllabi included sixty-five courses from 25 institutions in the following topic areas across disciplines:

- Women/feminist studies
- Sexuality
- Sexual abuse and domestic violence (generally in Pastoral Care)
- LGBT/queer issues

The syllabi review shows:

Few schools offer a comprehensive sexuality issues for religious professionals course. Such a course would provide a solid foundation for ministerial skills and/or personal formation across subject areas. A comprehensive course would include skill development in how to preach, counsel, educate, and advocate on sexuality-related issues. It would include content instruction so students were versed in their tradition's sacred texts, tradition/history, and denominational policies on sexuality issues. It would also provide an opportunity for students to reflect on their own sexual values, attitudes, and histories and include basic information on human sexuality, including sexual behaviors, sexual response, sexual orientation, gender identity, and personal relationships.

In contrast, most of the courses surveyed provide discipline-based training and lack the breadth required for adequate ministerial formation. For example, pastoral care and practical theology courses in sexuality-related issues most often require knowledge and practice of counseling skills, boundaries and limitations, and

preaching, but generally did not cover attraction or addressing sexual dysfunction. Theology courses focused on doctrinal development, while scripture courses focused on skill-building related to exegesis and awareness of particular interpretive frameworks. Ethics courses discussed professional boundaries, community rights, and commitments to inclusion. However, only four (6%) of the sexuality courses reviewed covered basic knowledge about human sexuality from a biological, physiological, or developmental perspective and few provided opportunities for personal reflection on sexual histories and attitudes. From a skills development perspective, in most seminaries, students would need to take a course (primarily offered as an elective) in each of the major disciplines with at least a course period on sexuality issues to acquire all the skills needed to be equipped as a sexually healthy religious professional.[32]

Most course designs and assigned readings reflect attention to intersecting social justice issues. In some cases, an entire course reflects a more direct approach to linking a particular community's understandings and experiences of sexuality-related issues (e.g., Gender, Race, and Class; Feminist Theologies in Third World Perspectives; Sexuality and the Black Church). More often, readings and various course designs signal attention to a variety of intersecting issues such as economics, environmental issues, racial/ethnic diversity, and disability issues.

Courses attend to a variety of similar topical areas relevant to sexuality issues regardless of discipline. For example, most courses address scriptural interpretation, traditions'/ histories' impact on current understandings of sexuality, issues of embodiment, formation of sexual relationships, and social construction of sexuality/resulting oppressions and abuse. Few address skills development in counseling, sexuality education, preaching, or social action. Less consistency exists in course design and primary assigned readings. For example, no two sexual ethics syllabi are

---

[32] The criteria for a sexually healthy religious professional are outlined in Debra Haffner (2002) *A Time to Build: Creating Sexually Healthy Faith Communities*, Westport, CT: Religious Institute on Sexual Morality, Justice, and Healing, or see pages 12 and 13.

the same. While one would expect to find variation given a faculty member's specialties and training, there are no identifiable core readings or jointly held interpretations of sexuality that seminary students taking these sexuality-related courses have in common across seminaries.

Forms of assessment and types of assignment do not contribute to practical ministerial skills. Assignments are most often completed in the form of papers or group presentations. With the exception of a few syllabi, the general objective of the papers and presentations is to synthesize course material, as opposed to translating course material into contexts of ministerial settings. Only a few courses tailored assignments to developing ministerial skills such as a paper on development of marriage doctrines in a theology course, ethical analysis of sexual abuse policies in faith communities in an ethics course, or one's professional role and possible interventions as a pastoral response to sexuality-related case studies.

We encourage all seminaries to use the Institutional Assessment to determine their institution's sexual health in the areas of curricular offerings, training opportunities, institutional environment including specific policies, and advocacy and support for sexuality-related issues.

Institutional Assessment

Criteria for a Sexually Healthy and Responsible Seminary

Check the box for each criterion your institution meets. Notice which areas need strengthening and develop plans to address them.

Curricular Offerings

A sexually healthy and responsible seminary:

☐ Requires coursework on human sexuality and healthy professional boundaries.

Offers regularly scheduled courses or workshops on sexuality issues, including:

☐ Sexual ethics

☐ LGBT/queer studies in religion

☐ Women in religious traditions and faith communities

☐ Sexual abuse and domestic violence

Includes sexuality topics in introductory and core courses:

☐ Hebrew Bible/Old Testament/Tanakh

☐ New Testament, Theology/Systematics

☐ Ethics

☐ History

☐ Midrash/Rabbinics/Code

☐ Pastoral Counseling

☐ Worship and Preaching

☐ Denomination-specific/polity classes

Graduating students are required to have:

☐ Opportunities for personal reflection on one's own sexuality

☐ Knowledge of human sexuality

☐ Ability to counsel, preach, educate, and advocate on sexuality issues in professional religious settings

Ideas for Next Steps

Few checked criteria in this area indicate the need for development of specific course offerings and integration of sexuality-related issues across curricular offerings. An institution may address this need through changes to degree program requirements, securing instructors for additional courses or workshops outside of current faculty specialties, and mandating syllabi that have a course design and required readings that address sexuality-related issues in at least one session in core introductory classes.

Training Opportunities

A sexually healthy and responsible seminary:

Requires training for doctoral students, junior faculty, and senior faculty on:

- ☐ human sexuality
- ☐ integrating sexuality issues into their training and courses
- ☐ advising students with diverse sexualities
- ☐ maintaining appropriate professional boundaries

Requires training for deans and administrative staff/advisors on:

- ☐ advising students with diverse sexualities
- ☐ maintaining appropriate professional boundaries

Ideas for Next Steps

Faculty and administrators serve students as teachers, advisors, and counselors. Training in professional boundaries and knowledge of diverse sexualities are integral to effective advising and first response counseling in academic institutions. Doctoral programs should require students be informed on sexuality-related issues in their teacher training. The next generation of scholars must also be exposed via coursework to sexuality-related research through curricular offerings. Faculty should be required to remain current on sexuality-related research in their field via workshops, campus events, and attendance at selected professional meetings.

Institutional Environment

A sexually healthy and responsible seminary:

- ☐ Holds worship opportunities that address sexuality issues.

Demonstrates a commitment to gender, racial/ethnic, and sexual diversity in the:

- ☐ student body
- ☐ faculty
- ☐ staff
- ☐ administrative leadership
- ☐ board of trustees

Has an inclusive language policy:

- ☐ For worship
- ☐ For print materials
- ☐ In the classroom

Offers library holdings that include current materials on sexuality and religion:

- ☐ Books published since 2000 on topics of sexuality and religion
- ☐ Curricula on sexuality education from denominations or independent presses
- ☐ Journals that specifically address a cross-section of sexuality and religion

Ideas for Next Steps

Many institutions and religious denominations have resources to assist in strengthening sexuality-related programs and policies. A minimum number of checked boxes indicates a need to develop more frequent opportunities and resources for students to engage sexuality issues. Many of the centers listed on pages 30-31 offer resources for worship services across religious traditions. The Religious Institute's website includes bibliographies of sexuality-related books, articles, and sexuality education curricula for libraries to reference and/or acquire. Model inclusive language policies can be acquired from other institutions or denominational bodies.

Policies

A sexually healthy and responsible seminary:

Has anti-discrimination and/or inclusion policies addressing:

- ☐ sex
- ☐ race
- ☐ disability
- ☐ sexual orientation
- ☐ gender identity
- ☐ marital status

☐ Includes anti-discrimination and/or inclusion policies in catalogs, admission materials, faculty and student orientations, websites, and periodic postings in newsletters and announcements.

Has sexual harassment prevention or professional ethics and healthy boundaries policies for:

- ☐ students
- ☐ faculty
- ☐ staff

☐ Includes sexual harassment policies and guidelines for reporting harassment in catalogs, admission materials, faculty and student orientations, websites, and periodic postings in newsletters and announcements.

Ideas for Next Steps

In some instances, there is a legal requirement to comply with anti-discrimination and sexual harassment policies. Seminaries should be aware of state and federal laws for educational institutions. When mandates do not exist, institutions can be proactive in creating policies that contribute to a safe and welcoming environment. The Religious Institute and the FaithTrust Institute assist seminaries in developing policies and provides training on professional ethics and healthy boundaries.

Advocacy and Support

A sexually healthy and responsible seminary:

Supports student groups that address sexual and gender identities and sexuality needs, such as:

- ☐ Women's Center
- ☐ LGBTQ groups
- ☐ Reproductive justice group
- ☐ Support for married/coupled seminarians
- ☐ HIV positive persons
- ☐ Single persons
- ☐ Celibate persons
- ☐ Other sexuality-related groups

Encourages faculty and leadership to be active on social and sexual justice issues including public witness and/or activism in:

- ☐ research and publications
- ☐ professional organizations
- ☐ advocacy organizations
- ☐ denomination settings
- ☐ community

Ideas for Next Steps

Institutions that do not have student groups or do not support specific sexuality-related groups should provide students with community-based references to organizations which can offer support such as Religious Coalition for Reproductive Choice regional affiliates, open and affirming congregations, or organizations such as Dignity and Lutherans Concerned. However, many students do not have time to seek support outside the institution. Faculty and administrative leadership in sexuality-related advocacy on a community, denominational, and professional society level should be recognized not only in the service requirement of tenure processes, but also as an avenue to supporting similar work within the seminary walls. Faculty and administrators can also serve as a religious voice in the public square on sexuality issues.

Opportunities and Recommendations for Action

A sexually healthy and responsible seminary promotes the integration of sexuality and spirituality across the curriculum, within the institutional environment, and through support and public advocacy for sexual justice issues. It makes a commitment to a sexual ethic based on equality and mutuality, not double standards. It requires an understanding that sexual integrity contributes to spiritual wholeness and is vital to ministerial formation.

The following five recommendations address needs highlighted by the *Sex and the Seminary* study and call upon the many partners involved and invested in the education of future religious leaders. Seminaries need the support of their denominational bodies, accrediting organizations, and each other to make significant strides in the sexual health of their institutions and of the professionals they graduate.

Opportunities & Recommendations

1. Require/develop competencies in sexuality for ordination.

2. Revise ministerial formation standards to include sexuality education.

3. Strengthen curricular offerings and seminary environment.

4. Invest in faculty development and continuing education.

5. Promote collaboration among seminaries, educational organizations, and advocacy groups.

Require/develop competencies in sexuality for ordination.

There can be no question that clergy must be sexually healthy religious professionals who possess the skills to address the sexuality needs of their congregants and maintain healthy ethical boundaries. Yet, as this study demonstrates, most seminaries are not providing their students with the opportunities to assess their own attitudes about sexuality or develop the skills they need. This is due, in part, to the fact that most denominations currently do not require their candidates for ministry to develop competencies in sexual health and education beyond sexual harassment prevention.

Denominational ordination bodies must begin to address the need for requirements and competencies for ordination with regard to sexuality-related skills. Competencies should demonstrate that candidates are "comfortable with their own sexuality, [have] the skills to provide pastoral care and worship on sexuality issues, and [are] committed to sexual justice in the congregation and the society at large."[33] During preparation for ordination, candidates should be required to complete courses or workshops on sexual health, education, and counseling. Denominational bodies can use their own education offices to develop specific curricula in conjunction with seminaries in order to provide learning opportunities.

We support and encourage denominations to develop or arrange educational trainings on sexuality issues grounded in their faith tradition. The Religious Institute can provide assistance to denominational offices as they establish competency guidelines. Denominational leadership in collaboration with seminaries can create a sustainable change in the sexuality training candidates for ordination receive.

2

Revise ministerial formation standards to include sexuality education.

The Association of Theological Schools should require that seminaries integrate sexuality education into ministerial formation.[34] Current ATS standards require seminaries to "take into account: knowledge of the religious heritage; understanding of the cultural context; growth in spiritual depth and moral integrity; and capacity for ministerial and public leadership."[35] Sexuality-related issues are present in each of these four areas and should be addressed explicitly in ministerial formation:

Religious Heritage: Through coursework in scriptural, historical, theological, and denominational/polity studies, institutions can provide structured opportunities for students to learn how scripture and the historical tradition have shaped the understanding of sexual ethics, denominational policy, and attention or lack of attention to these issues.

Cultural Context: In disciplines such as ethics, systematic theology, practical theology, and religious education, students should have opportunities "to develop an understanding of the cultural realities and structures" related to sexuality issues within the life of their particular faith community and society at large. In particular, students need to develop an awareness of and sensitivity to the rapidly changing context of sexuality and gender identity. In addition, it is important for students to reflect on how diverse racial and ethnic cultures and variations in religious traditions have affected their own sexualities and those of the people they will be called to serve.

---

[33] Haffner, Debra W. (2001). *A Time to Build: Creating Sexually Healthy Faith Communities*, Westport, CT: Religious Institute on Sexual Morality, Justice, and Healing, 14.
[34] The Association of Theological Schools is the accrediting body for Christian, Unitarian Universalist and non-denominational/inter-denominational Christian seminaries. Jewish colleges and seminaries represented in this survey are accredited by regional commissions on higher education (e.g., The Jewish Theological School is accredited by Middle States Commission on Higher Education).
[35] The Association of Theological Schools (2006) "Degree Program Standards," Bulletin 47, Part 1, Standard A, section A.2.0. Pittsburgh, PA. The following four areas of Program Content are taken from *Bulletin 47*, Standard A, Section A.3.1.1-4.

Personal and Spiritual Formation: Religious professionals in training must have opportunities to assess how their sexuality affects their "personal faith, emotional maturity, moral integrity, and public witness." Such an assessment requires knowledge about human sexuality, including sexual behaviors, sexual response, sexual orientation, gender identity, and personal relationships, as well as theological reflection on the integration of sexuality and spirituality. It also includes an examination of how religious influences have affected their own sexuality, reflections on their own sexual biographies, and awareness of these effects on others.

Capacity for Ministerial and Public Leadership: Students must understand their own denominational policies on sexuality-related issues and current movements

for sexual justice in order to "cultivate the capacity for leadership in both ecclesial and public contexts." Students should have opportunities to develop the skills to preach and counsel on sexuality-related issues. In addition, they should develop conflict resolution and negotiation skills on divisive subjects. They should be encouraged to develop advocacy skills, including public speaking and media training, in order to present theologically informed viewpoints in the public square.

The Association of Theological Schools (ATS) and other accrediting bodies must work collaboratively with institutional representatives to further articulate how sexuality-related issues can become part of the standards for theological education. As part of this effort, the Religious Institute will distribute this report to every seminary in the U.S. The Religious Institute will also work with ATS member schools as they advocate for changes in and contribute to revisions of the ATS Standards for Accreditation scheduled for 2012.

=============== 3 ===============

Strengthen curricular offerings and seminary environment.

Seminaries must not only offer, but also require, the coursework that religious professionals will need to address the sexuality-related issues that arise in ministry. This coursework might include a combination of full-semester courses, coverage in introductory courses, and credit and non-credit workshops. These educational opportunities must be regularly scheduled and built into degree requirements. The seminary representatives who were part of this project recommend "required coursework on human sexuality and healthy professional boundaries." A sexually healthy and responsible seminary will require at least one course on sexuality for graduation, a requirement that only one of the 36 seminaries we studied currently has.

Seminaries also must assure a supportive environment for sexuality-related issues. Seminaries must have anti-discrimination, sexual harassment, and full inclusion policies that reflect sexual and gender diversities. It was a welcome surprise that almost 9 out of the 10 seminaries have anti-discrimination policies that include sexual orientation, and half have such policies for transgender students, staff, and faculty; other seminaries, unless prohibited by their faith traditions, should implement such policies. In addition, seminaries must provide opportunities for worship and advocacy that reflect the diversity of sexuality issues students will encounter in their ministry.

Seminaries also must address gender equity in their faculties, staff, and boards of trustees. Although most of the schools report increasing numbers of women students (and in some seminaries, women now constitute more than half of the student population), there is an unyielding stained glass ceiling in leadership. Women represent only 19% of the presidents and 42% of the deans in the seminaries studied. Even more surprisingly, only 28% of the seminaries have boards of trustees with at least 40% women in leadership. This continued male dominance in leadership, especially on the governing boards, does not reflect the change in student composition in the past twenty years and can easily be addressed through identification and recruitment of qualified women.

4

Invest in faculty development and continuing education.

Too often, faculty members who teach sexuality or LGBT courses report feeling isolated in their own seminaries. Program units at the American Academy of Religion are generally more likely to concentrate on theoretical issues of queer theology or the aesthetics of sexuality than on sexuality issues related to ministry. To improve their effectiveness in training future religious professionals, faculty members who offer courses on sexuality-related issues require ongoing development opportunities and supportive networks for resource sharing. These resources should be made available to doctoral students as well.

To contribute to faculty development in sexuality education, the Religious Institute has committed to:

- Develop a faculty network for sharing bibliographies and syllabi, including faith-based community resources and pedagogy.
- Collaborate with sexual and reproductive health organizations to provide training opportunities in human sexuality and sexuality education at regional seminary locations (Boston Theological Union, Graduate Theological Union at Berkeley, and in Atlanta, Chicago, and New York).
- Conduct workshops and outreach at professional meetings, such as the American Academy of Religion, Society for Biblical Literature, etc. (AAR, SBL, SCE/SJE, Society for Pastoral Theology, and Association of Professors, Practitioners and Researchers in Religious Education).

Continuing education is necessary to fill the gap in preparation and training for those currently serving in ministerial roles. Seminaries might consider continuing education for alumni at reunions or satellite events, or on-campus workshops open to religious professionals in the community. For example, Union Theological Seminary will host its annual alumni gathering in October 2009 on the topic of "Sex in the Church," highlighting current research in sexuality and religion, discussion of denominational action on sexuality-related issues, and training opportunities for alumni. Organizations such as the Alban Institute, Auburn Seminary, and universities with sexual health doctoral programs can also work with the Religious Institute to offer clergy in-service training on these issues.

5

Promote collaboration among seminaries, educational organizations, and advocacy groups.

Given the financial constraints at many institutions, no seminary can be expected to do all of this on its own.[36]

------

[36] See "Seminary Distress" in *The Christian Century*, 125(9) (2008), 7.

In order to invest in the sexual health of seminary students and their future congregations, there need to be resource-rich partnerships. These partnerships would allow for jointly developed courses, workshops, and other educational events. A number of centers now provide resources that complement and reinforce what individual seminaries can offer, including regional events, worship materials, bibliographies, and trainings. Seminaries should explore additional opportunities for collaboration.

Local collaboration is already taking place and should be further encouraged between institutions that are within a Union or have regional school affiliates. For example, students at other schools within the Graduate Theological Union at Berkeley can join the Pacific School of Religion's certificate program in sexuality. These institutions already offer workshops and events and open their classes to students from other institutions.

Seminaries, denominational offices, and accrediting bodies can benefit from advocacy and educational organizations that provide faith-based resources and trainings, as well as ongoing support for students as they move into professional ministry careers. For more information on organizations which provide continuing education and technical assistance on sexuality from a faith-based perspective, see the resource list on page 48.

Closing Words

Seminaries nurture, educate, and train the next generation of clergy and religious professionals. Theological education cannot afford to neglect sexuality education and training for religious professionals and clergy. At a time when virtually every major religious movement is wrestling with issues of gender inequity, teen sexuality, and the rights of LGBT persons, many denominations have no requirement for sexuality education and training for their future clergy. In an age when sexuality permeates popular culture, and reproductive choice, sex education, and marriage equality headline the nation's political discourse, seminaries are not prioritizing sexuality-related courses or integrating sexuality training within ministerial formation. In a profession that finds individuals and couples, families and communities turning to them for guidance and counseling, substantial numbers of religious professionals report that their seminary training did not prepare them to address the diverse sexuality issues that arise in ministry.

Religious professionals and clergy must be able to deal with sexuality issues on personal, pastoral, and denominational levels. We have heard the witness of those who have been abused, neglected, or marginalized for reasons of sexual orientation, gender, and gender identity. We have seen how sexual misconduct and sexual abuse scar individuals, tear congregations apart, and financially devastate and ethically discredit denominational bodies. Theological education can no longer afford to neglect sexuality education and training for religious professionals and clergy.

Many partners are needed to bridge the gap between sexuality and the seminary. Collaboration among seminaries, denomination offices, accrediting bodies, and education and advocacy groups is necessary to assure that every theological institution is a sexually healthy and responsible one. Through commitment and collaboration, we can change the landscape of sexuality education for religious professionals and clergy. Together, we can assure that future religious leaders will indeed be pastors for sexual health and prophets for sexual justice.

References Cited

Aleshire, D.O. (2003). "What Matters in Good MDiv Curricula?" Presented at the Consultation on Designing MDiv Curriculum, The Association of Theological Schools.

Aleshire, D.O. (2008). *Earthen Vessels: Hopeful Reflections on the Work and Future of Theological Schools.* Grand Rapids, MI: Wm. B. Eerdmans Publishing Company.

The Association of Theological Schools (2006). "Degree Program Standards," *Bulletin 47*, Pittsburgh, PA.

Brichard, T. (2000). "Clergy Sexual Misconduct: Frequency and Causation." *Sexual and Relationship Therapy* 15(2).

The Center for Sexuality and Religion (2002). Section: The Role of Sexuality Education Within Seminaries in *The Case for Comprehensive Sexuality Education Within the Context of Seminary Human and Theological Formation: A Report of the Ford Foundation,* Philadelphia, PA. Clapp, S, et al. (2002). *Faith Matters.* Fort Wayne, IN: Christian Community/LifeQuest.

Conklin, S.C. (2001). Seminary Sexuality Education Survey: Current Efforts, Perceived Need and Readiness in Accredited Christian Institutions. *Journal of Sex Education and Therapy* 26 (4).

Conklin, S.C. (2000). "Six Billion and Counting Compel Sexuality Study in Churches." *The Clergy Journal* 76(6).

Editors (May 6, 2008). "Seminary Distress." *The Christian Century* 125(9), 7.

Ellison, C.G. & Goodson, P. (1997). "Conservative Protestantism and attitudes toward family planning in a sample of seminarians." *Journal for the Scientific Study of Religion* 36(4).

Fortune, M.M. (1991). *Is Nothing Sacred? When Sex Invades the Pastoral Relationship.* San Francisco: Harper.
Friesen, D.H. (1988). Sex Education in the Seminary Setting: Its Effects on Attitudes, Knowledge, and Counseling Responses. Doctoral Dissertation, The University of Iowa, Ames, IA.

Haffner, D.W. (2001). *A Time to Build: Creating Sexually Healthy Faith Communities.* Westport, CT: Religious Institute on Sexual Morality, Justice, and Healing.

Heyward, C. (2003). "We're Here, We're Queer: Teaching Sex in Seminary." *Body and Soul: Rethinking Sexuality as Justice Love*, eds. Marvin Ellison and Sylvia Thorson-Smith, Cleveland: Pilgrim Press.

Hough, J.C., Jr. (1995). "Future Pastors, Future Church: The Seminary Quarrels." *The Christian Century* 112(18).

King, G.B. (1995). "Trends in Seminary Education," in K. B. Bedell (Ed.), *Yearbook of American & Canadian Churches* Nashville, TN: Abingdon Press.

Johnson, F.B. et al. (1986). "Ask the Churches about Faith and Sexuality: A UCC Survey of Needs for Program Development." Unpublished report presented to the United Church Board for Homeland Ministries.

Lebacqz, K. & Barton, R. (1991). *Sex in the Parish.* Louisville: Westminister/John Knox Press.

Meek, K.R., et al. (2004). "Sexual Ethics Training in Seminary: Preparing Students to Manage Feelings of Sexual Attraction." *Pastoral Psychology* 53(1).

Palmer, T., et al. (2007). *A Time to Seek: Study Guide on Sexual and Gender Diversity*, Westport, CT: Religious Institute on Sexual Morality, Justice, and Healing.

Palmer, T., et al. (2008). "Survey of Religious Progres-sives." Westport, CT: Religious Institute on Sexual Morality, Justice, and Healing.

Pan American Health Organization (2001). *Promotion of Sexual Health. Recommendations for Action* (Washington, DC: PAHO).

Pope, K.S., Sonne, J.L., and Holroyd, J. (1993). *Sexual Feelings in Psychotherapy: Explorations of Therapists and Therapists-in-training*. Washington, DC: American Psychological Association.

Presbyterian Church, U.S.A. (1991). Presbyterians and Human Sexuality: The 203rd General Assembly Response to the Report of the Special Committee on Human Sexu-ality, Including a "Minority Report." Louisville, KY: Office of the General Assembly, Presbyterian Church (USA).

Richards, D.E. (1992). "Issues of Religion, Sexual Adjustment, and the Role of the Pastoral Counselor" in R. M. Green (Ed.), *Religion and Sexual Health: Ethical, Theological, and Critical Perspectives*. Norwell, MA: Kluwer Academic Publishers.

Robinson, L.H. (2004). "The Abuse of Power: A View of Sexual Misconduct in a Systemic Approach to Pastoral Care." *Pastoral Psychology* 52(5).

Schmidt, K. (2002). "Moving Beyond Fear." *Yale Medicine*, Winter 2002. Yale University School of Medicine.

Schuth, K. (1999). *Seminaries, Theologates, and the Future of Church Ministry: An Analysis of Trends and Transitions*. Collegeville, MN: The Liturgical Press.

Weiderman, M.W., & Sansone, R.A. (1999). "Sexual-ity Training for Professional Psychologists: A National Survey of Training Directors in Doctoral Programs and Predoctoral Internships." *Professional Psychology: Research and Practice* 30(3).

Resources

Leading Seminaries on Sexuality Criteria

Andover Newton Theological School
210 Herrick Road
Newton Centre, MA 02459
http://www.ants.edu

Candler School of Theology, Emory University
1531 Dickey Drive
Atlanta, GA 30322
http://www.candler.emory.edu

Chicago Theological Seminary
5757 S. University Avenue
Chicago, IL 60637
http://www.ctschicago.edu

Claremont School of Theology
1325 N. College Avenue
Claremont, CA 91711
http://www.cst.edu

Drew Theological School, Drew University
36 Madison Avenue
Madison, NJ 07940
http://www.drew.edu/theo

Episcopal Divinity School
99 Brattle Street
Cambridge, MA 02138
http://www.eds.edu

Harvard University Divinity School
45 Francis Avenue
Cambridge, MA 02138
http://www.hds.harvard.edu

Reconstructionist Rabbinical College
1299 Church Road
Wyncote, PA 19095
http://www.rrc.edu

Vanderbilt University Divinity School
411 21st Avenue South
Nashville, TN 37240-1121
http://www.vanderbilt.edu/divinity

Wake Forest University School of Divinity
1834 Wake Forest Road
Winston-Salem, NC 27106
http://www.divinity.wfu.edu

Sexuality Training

Religious Institute on Sexual Morality, Justice, & Healing
21 Charles Street, Suite 140
Westport, CT 06880
http://www.religiousinstitute.org
info@religiousinstute.org

FaithTrust Institute
2400 N. 45th Street #101
Seattle, WA 98103
http://www.faithtrustinstitute.org
operations@faithtrustinstitute.org

Theology and Reproductive Choice: A Seminary Syllabus
Human Sexuality Webinars: Black Church Initiative
Religious Coalition for Reproductive Choice
1025 Vermont Avenue NW, Suite 1130
Washington, DC 20005
http://www.rcrc.org